SUCCESS IN SCHOOL

The Essential How-To Guide for Students of All Ages

SUSAN H. ANDRES AND FELICITY PINE

ROWMAN & LITTLEFIELD EDUCATION

A division of
ROWMAN & LITTLEFIELD PUBLISHERS, INC.
Lanham • New York • Toronto • Plymouth, UK

Copyright

This book was placed by the Educational Design Services LLC literary agency.
Published by Rowman & Littlefield Education
A division of Rowman & Littlefield Publishers, Inc.
A wholly owned subsidiary of The Rowman & Littlefield Publishing Group, Inc.
4501 Forbes Boulevard, Suite 200, Lanham, Maryland 20706
www.rowman.com

10 Thornbury Road, Plymouth PL6 7PP, United Kingdom

British Library Cataloguing in Publication Information Available

Library of Congress Cataloging-in-Publication Data

Andres, Susan H., 1949–
   Success in school : the essential how-to guide for students of all ages / Susan H. Andres and Felicity Pine.
      p. cm.
   Summary: "Success in School is a teaching tool, how-to guide, and reference manual that will support students throughout their school careers"—Provided by publisher.
   Includes bibliographical references.
   ISBN 978-1-61048-307-0 (pbk.)—ISBN 978-1-61048-308-7 (electronic)
   1. Study skills—Handbooks, manuals, etc. 2. Study environment—Handbooks, manuals, etc. 3. Students—Time management—Handbooks, manuals, etc. I. Pine, Felicity, 1950– II. Title.
   LB1049.P464 2012
   371.3028'1—dc23   2011048601

∞™ The paper used in this publication meets the minimum requirements of American National Standard for Information Sciences—Permanence of Paper for Printed Library Materials, ANSI/NISO Z39.48-1992.

Printed in the United States of America

The authors acknowledge permission to reprint excerpts from the following:

From *THE AMERICAN NATION* Copyright © 1991, 1989, 1986 Pearson Education, Inc., or its affiliates. Used by permission. All Rights Reserved.

From *CAVE BOY* by Cathy East Dubowski and Mark Dubowski, copyright © 1988 by Cathy East Dubowski and Mark Dubowski. Used by permission of Random House Children's Books, a division of Random House, Inc.

From *DINASAUR DAYS* by Joyce Milton, copyright © 1985 by Joyce Milton. Used by permission of Random House Children's Books, a division of Random House, Inc.

From *MAGIC ELIZABETH* by Norma Kassirer, Scholastic Book Services, 1966. Reproduced with permission from Norma Kassirer.

From *NORMA JEAN, JUMPING BEAN* by Joanna Cole, copyright © 1987 by Joanna Cole. Used by permission of Random House Children's Books, a division of Random House, Inc.

From *SCIENCE EXPLORER: ENVIRONMENTAL SCIENCE* Copyright © 2000 Pearson Education, Inc., or its affiliates. Used by permission. All Rights Reserved.

From *SCIENCEPLUS: Technology and Society,* Student Edition. Copyright © 1993 by Holt, Rinehart and Winston, Inc. All rights reserved. Reproduced by permission of the publisher, Houghton Mifflin Harcourt Publishing Company.

From *THE STORY OF AMERICA,* Student Edition. Copyright © 1994 by Holt, Rinehart and Winston, Inc. All rights reserved. Reproduced by permission of the publisher, Houghton Mifflin Harcourt Publishing Company.

Reprinted with the permission of Simon & Schuster, Inc. from *THE ROAD LESS TRAVELED* by M. Scott Peck, M.D. Copyright © 1978 M. Scott Peck.

Table of Contents

Preface

Susan Andres

Susan Andres, M.Ed., a learning specialist for more than twenty-five years, has taught study strategies to students at all grade levels and witnessed significant improvement in their schoolwork. Although her career has been gratifying, she was frustrated to think that she could help only a handful of young people. Her decision to write a book brought her together with writer/designer Felicity Pine, M.A., who is also a tutor and seasoned school communications administrator. As co-authors, they have produced a practical manual that outlines a concise set of proven teaching methods, incorporating relevant examples and student samples, in an appealing, easy-to-follow format.

Felicity Pine

This book is a "how-to," reference, and guide to the learning, writing, and organizational strategies necessary to navigate school successfully. Users can focus on individual chapters as needed or skip around within a chapter. The writing is directed toward adults – parents, teachers, tutors – who want to help students, and while older students can understand and apply these strategies on their own, they may still need adult assistance.* The goal is to provide a foundation for learning that will foster independence. To that end, the rewards are many: improved self-esteem, higher grades, and skills that can be practiced for a lifetime.

Students deserve to feel the satisfaction of a positive educational experience. The authors encourage parents and other adults to help students learn and practice the study skills they need to enjoy success in school.

*Please note that learning styles differ and each grade level presents special challenges. Adapt this guide to individual needs.

Acknowledgements

SUSAN ANDRES

My idea for this book came after working with countless young people as a learning and reading specialist. I wanted to reach more students than my private practice allowed by compiling some of my ideas, principles, and strategies into a study guide. When I met Felicity, my modest dream became a reality greater than I could have imagined. Her immense contribution to content, design, and writing is equal only to her loyalty. From New York, where we met and made the decision to write this book together, to Tennessee, Massachusetts, and finally to Pennsylvania, where we completed the last chapter, Felicity and I have shared more than just a professional relationship. We journeyed together through personal crises, family triumphs, debilitating illnesses, and new beginnings. Miraculously, through it all, we persisted and now realize the fruits of our long labor.

Without the support and input of many, this book would not have found its way. I'd like to thank my former husband, Bill Andres, for his unending encouragement and patience. I continually appreciate my father, Marvin Hirschhorn, for his generosity, good humor, and support and my mother, Gloria Hirschhorn, for her steadfast love, faith in me, and discerning mind. Along with their affection, I credit my sister and brother-in-law, Carrie and Steve Sherretta, with invaluable professional perspective. Many thanks to my brother, Rick Hirschhorn, for his expert business counsel and always being there when we needed him. I am deeply indebted to Dr. Jonathan Grayson for his profound insight, without which I would have no appreciation for the gift of life. Last but not least, thank you to my honey, Don Rassler, for being by and on my side.

I am especially grateful for my relationship with colleague and mentor Dianne Forman, whose guidance and influence helped me to establish myself as a reading specialist. I am also privileged to have worked with Dr. Irene Gaskins, who has made major contributions to the fields of reading and cognition. She provided me with the skills needed to implement strategy instruction, the foundation of my teaching techniques.

I am much obliged to the many children who crossed my professional path for making me a better teacher. Finally, I would like to acknowledge the following students who supplied us with their invaluable schoolwork, so we could feature real student samples in our book: Abigale, Alex, Arjun, Blythe, Brian, Daniel, Greg, Katie H, Katie P, Marde, Michael P, Michael S, Michele, Morgan, Murray, Rachel F, Rachel M, and Rachel O.

FELICITY PINE

Along with the above acknowledgments, I must single out my husband, Jim, who has watched me produce a plethora of persuasive publicity for others and always wanted me to create something for myself. I am indebted to my children, Katherine and Michael, for sharing their own multifaceted school experiences with me and allowing us to use their schoolwork as samples. I appreciate the devotion and forbearance of my parents and brothers, who have had to sacrifice family time to the production of this tome. Most of all, I want to recognize Susan for her strength, perseverance, and profound friendship.

This book is dedicated to our kids: Aubrey Zoe, Liza Skye, Benjamin Joseph, Michael Rudolph, and Katherine Anna.

"Why should I try? I won't do well anyway."

Skill development is only part of the secret to success. The willingness to try is the key component. This section recommends some motivational techniques that can help build self-esteem and cultivate a satisfying school experience.

1. Play a <u>positive role</u>.

- Be <u>optimistic</u>. Students who have a positive attitude are more likely to take responsibility for their schoolwork and enjoy the rewards of success.

- Students are receptive to <u>positive feedback</u> and often resistant to negative remarks.

- Recognize the good points before offering <u>constructive criticism</u>. Then make a suggestion that could improve the final product:

  "Your paper shows that you've really researched your subject. Reading it has made me feel like an expert on the North American bison. I did notice a few grammatical errors that I circled for you. Could you proofread again?"

- Speak in ways that sound <u>nonthreatening</u>. Avoid a preaching or lecturing tone, and keep it simple.

- Be <u>specific</u> when offering praise:

  "I like your title. It cleverly previews your thesis."

- Guide students. Avoid pushing solutions. Ask <u>questions</u> that can help them solve problems. It is important for students to take ownership of their work:

  "Do you need any help with your multiplication tables? How could I test you on them?"

- Underscore the good feelings of accomplishment but also <u>acknowledge frustration</u> if it occurs:

  "I can tell that you're feeling frustrated. Let's think about how you can get back on track."

2. Have <u>fun</u>.

- Show the student – by modeling a <u>positive attitude</u> – that learning can be fun and rewarding.

- Use <u>humor</u> to deflect frustration. Divert attention from a disheartening situation.

- Discuss a school responsibility <u>informally</u>. For example, brainstorm ideas over lunch before the student begins to work on an oral report.

- Adding a <u>social</u> component to schoolwork can boost morale: studying with a friend, working in a library, setting up a study group.

  (For more about study groups: Step 10)

- Positive <u>reinforcement</u> can also help motivate the reluctant student. The promise of a <u>reward</u> can be an effective tool. Eventually, personal accomplishment becomes its own reward.

  (For more about positive reinforcement: Step 7)

3. Take a <u>break</u>.

- Before frustration overwhelms the student, take a break and resume schoolwork later.

- <u>Mirror</u> the student's feelings and <u>model</u> a solution:

  "Wow, this book report takes a lot of concentration. Maybe we should stop for awhile. Let's plan breaks that we can take if we need them."

- Encourage more independent students to build in breaks to make the work more manageable.
- A <u>physical activity</u> is a nice contrast to a mental one, or stop and make a <u>healthy snack</u> to refresh the body as well as the mind.
- After a short break, the student should be able to concentrate again. If frustration continues, explore what the problem could be.
- If trouble with schoolwork persists, seek professional help.

4. <u>Model</u> the thinking process.

- Students need to learn how to think through a concept in order to understand it.
- An effective way to teach this skill is to model the process: <u>Think out loud</u>.
- Try to break down and <u>verbalize the steps</u> that are involved in thinking.
  See Sample A.

Sample: Model the Thinking Process

A: Reviewing Cause and Effect – Primary Reader

READING SELECTION: *This dinosaur was fat and slow. It could not run and hide. But it did not need to! Its back was covered with thick plates. Its tail was covered with sharp spikes. Its name was Stegosaurus (STEG-uh-SOR-us). That means "covered lizard." It was one of the early dinosaurs.*

– Joyce Milton, <u>Dinosaur Days</u>

"We are going to find examples of cause and effect in this story about a dinosaur.

[MODELING CONCEPT OF CAUSE AND EFFECT] But first, if I don't remember the meaning of cause and effect, I will think back to our lesson about sunlight, rain, and flowers. We talked about sunlight and rain helping to make flowers grow. So sunlight and rain are the cause, and flowers are the effect. In other words, sunlight and rain cause flowers to grow.

I often try to use something I know to help me understand something new.

Remember that in real time a cause comes before an effect, but in a sentence, we can reverse the order and mean the same thing: Flowers grow because they get sunlight and rain.

Read about the Stegosaurus, and find an example of cause and effect."

5. Encourage <u>decision making</u>.

- We all have to make decisions in our everyday lives – from simple to complex and with varying consequences.
- Throughout their school experiences, students are faced with decision-making dilemmas, many of which can have a major effect on their lives.
- Empower students to make thoughtful decisions.

- An effective decision-making process is known as SODAS, which stands for <u>S</u>ituation, <u>O</u>ptions, <u>D</u>isadvantages, <u>A</u>dvantages, and <u>S</u>olution:

S = Identify the <u>Situation</u>.

What is the <u>problem</u>? Discuss the <u>facts</u> of the situation. What are the student's <u>feelings</u>? What are the feelings of others whom she may need to consider?

O = Brainstorm the <u>Options</u>.

What <u>choices</u> does the student have to resolve this problem? Sometimes the options are given, such as a list of possible after-school clubs from which to choose. At other times, the student has to come up with options: themes for a party, for example.

D = Examine the <u>Disadvantages</u>.

A = Explore the <u>Advantages</u>.

Before considering the disadvantages and advantages of an option, <u>research</u> may be necessary. The student may have to look objectively at her strengths, weaknesses, and values.

For example, let's say the student is thinking of joining the Drama Club, but she is uncomfortable speaking in front of a group. When considering the pros and cons of this option, her "weakness" could be regarded as a disadvantage. On the other hand, joining the drama club could be a way to confront and overcome her fear – an advantage.

S = Choose the <u>Solution</u>.

Ask <u>questions</u> that can trigger useful responses. For example, does she know or can she find out about the schedule of drama club performances? Can she manage that schedule?

<u>Summarize</u> the relevant points. Help her weigh the <u>consequences</u> of different choices and understand why one might be better for her than another.

After the student examines the options, their disadvantages and advantages, she makes her <u>decision</u>.

- <u>Follow up</u> with the student:

Ask if she has implemented her decision. For example, has she signed up for the club activity of her choice? If not, ask whether she was unsure of her choice. Discuss it further.

If the student has implemented her decision, engage her in a conversation about the outcome. Is she satisfied with her choice? If not, help her select another option, and affirm the importance of persistence.

On the other hand, if she is not permitted to change her decision, encourage her to focus on the positive and make the best of the circumstance.

- Introduce the process of decision making at an early age. Just modify the language and simplify the steps. ***See Sample B.***

Sample: Decision Making

B: SODAS Worksheet – Middle School

SITUATION
- I can't decide what to do this summer.
- My best friend wants me to go to her camp for 8 wks. She's so excited, and it sounds like fun.
- I've been thinking about going to a soccer camp for 3 wks, and I really want to do that too.
- My parents want me to go to the soccer camp.

OPTIONS
1) I can go to the same camp as my best friend for 8 wks.
2) I can go to the soccer camp for 3 wks.

DISADVANTAGES
1) Best friend's camp
   - I won't get to play soccer, which I really like to do, and I won't improve my skills.
   - My parents will be upset even though they are letting me make my own decision.
   - I won't have time to do things with my family and other friends because it's a lot of time away (plus a lot of money).
2) Soccer camp
   - I won't see my best friend all summer.
   - She'll probably be mad at me.
   - I'll have too much free time after camp is over.

ADVANTAGES
1) Best friend's camp
   - I'll be with my best friend all summer.
   - She'll really be happy.
   - I'll have a whole summer of fun activities.
2) Soccer camp
   - I really, really love soccer, and I'll be playing a lot.
   - I'll improve my soccer skills.
   - My parents will be happy.
   - When I'm back home after 3 wks, I can plan other activities like going to the pool and movies, and I can do workouts.

SOLUTION
I'm choosing soccer camp for 3 main reasons:
   - I really love playing soccer.
   - I want to improve my skills because I plan to play in high school and maybe college.
   - My friend knows how important soccer is to me, and if she's a real friend, she won't be too angry about my decision.

FOLLOW UP
____
____
____
____

6. Collaborate.

- If the student is making a <u>genuine effort</u> but a task is taking its toll, step in and help out.
- Whether helping an eight-year-old to put away his games or an eighteen-year-old to complete his college application, <u>adult involvement</u> can avert frustration and model desirable behavior. Read together, test him during the final stage of studying, offer to make the call to schedule a college visit.
- At the same time, doing his work for him is not constructive. Teachers must be aware of their students' strengths and weaknesses, and students must become independent workers.

7. Use <u>behavior modification</u> wisely.

- <u>Positive reinforcement programs</u> can help change behaviors that interfere with a student's progress.

- Promising a <u>reward</u> (stickers, certificates of achievement, special activities) can motivate the reluctant student to accomplish a task. Try to implement <u>incentives</u> before frustration mounts.

- Establish a goal – the <u>desired behavior</u>. Keep in mind that mastering a major skill area involves acquiring component skills. Make sure to establish <u>incremental goals</u> along the way – not too easy, not too hard.

- <u>Negotiate</u> the reward, so the student is involved and willing to participate.

- The kind of reward chosen is ultimately the adult's decision and depends upon the family's <u>values</u> and <u>circumstances</u>.

- Select the <u>smallest and most meaningful reward</u> that is effective. For example, if a new school supply is sufficient, avoid offering a video game.

- Behavior modification programs range from unstructured plans, such as the use of <u>stickers</u>, to structured plans, such as the use of <u>behavior charts</u>.

- A behavior chart consists of a written goal and spaces for recording the student's <u>progress</u> (checks, stars, smiley faces). A designated number of stars, for example, can be "cashed in" later for a more significant reward.

- The easier a behavior modification program is to implement, the more likely it will work.

- Limit the use of gifts as a reward. <u>Activities</u>, such as a family basketball game or a sleepover with a friend, are often more appropriate.

- A compelling reward may simply acknowledge an accomplished task – a <u>certificate</u> that highlights the student's achievement, for example. This kind of reinforcement helps to promote learning for learning's sake.

- When a reward is given, <u>verbalize the accomplishment</u>:

  "Congratulations. You worked on your notecards every day this week. Now, you can watch the movie you've wanted to see."

- Some students may need to be rewarded immediately after a task is completed, while others may be able to wait. Determine the <u>specific time frame</u> that works effectively.

- Make sure the student understands what is expected. Before the program begins, discuss and agree to the terms. Perhaps have the student sign a simple <u>contract</u>.

- Once the student is developing the desired skill and experiencing success, the behavior modification program may be <u>gradually discontinued</u>. Increase the time spent on a given task, increase the number of tasks that must be completed without the help of a parent, and provide incentives randomly to decrease the student's expectations and dependency on external rewards.

- <u>Spoken praise</u> and <u>gestures of approval</u> are the most natural external rewards. They can greatly reinforce positive behavior and lead to feelings of self-worth. Be specific and identify the task done well. Remember to praise effort, too. At the same time, be discriminating. Use praise only when it is deserved, and do not go overboard:

  "I think your essay is quite persuasive. Your writing has really developed this year. May I have a copy to show your grandparents?"

- When the student experiences <u>success</u> and recognizes her own <u>ability</u>, she has acquired the most valuable reward.

Motivation

- <u>Avoid punishment</u>, which can deflate self-esteem and spark feelings of anger and resentment. Especially avoid taking away meaningful activities that can build skills and self-confidence (sports, music, community service).
- If a student continues to struggle, <u>consult a specialist</u>. Professional intervention can help cultivate success in school.
  See Samples C & D.

C. Behavior Chart – Math

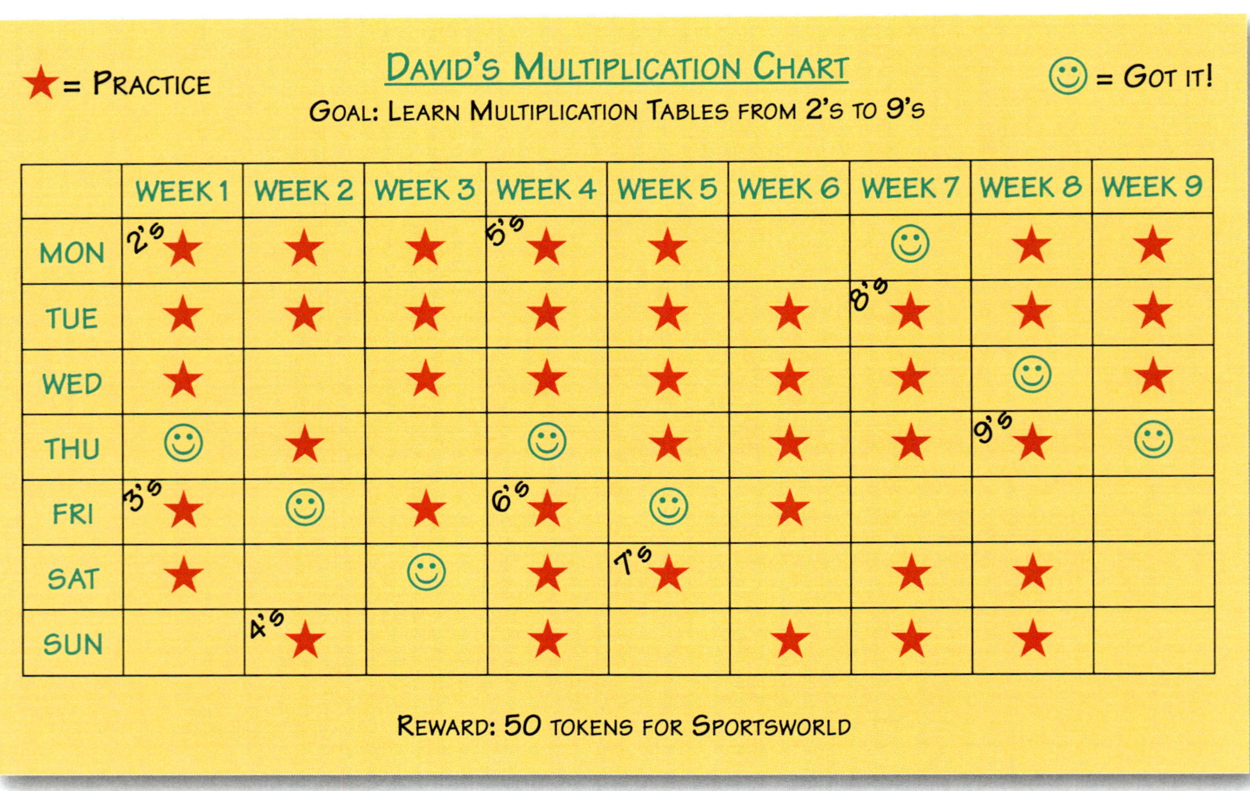

	WEEK 1	WEEK 2	WEEK 3	WEEK 4	WEEK 5	WEEK 6	WEEK 7	WEEK 8	WEEK 9
MON	2's ★	★	★	5's ★	★		☺	★	★
TUE	★	★	★	★	★	★	8's ★	★	★
WED	★	★	★	★	★	★	★	☺	★
THU	☺	★		☺	★	★	★	9's ★	☺
FRI	3's ★	☺	★	6's ★	☺	★			
SAT	★		☺	★	7's ★		★	★	
SUN		4's ★		★		★	★	★	

D. Behavior Chart – Reading

SOPHIE'S READING CHART
READING FOR PLEASURE

GOAL: READ AN AVERAGE OF 20 MINUTES PER DAY IN THE MONTH OF APRIL (600 MINUTES)

	APRIL 1	APRIL 8	APRIL 15	APRIL 22	APRIL 29
MONDAY	15	20	0	20	15
TUESDAY	20	20	15	30	20
WEDNESDAY	0	0	20	20	
THURSDAY	20	15	15	30	
FRIDAY	30	0	0	60	
SATURDAY	60	30	90	30	
SUNDAY	0	90	90	30	

WOW!!!

TOTAL: 145 + 175 + 230 + 220 + 35 = 805

REWARD: 6-GIRL SLEEPOVER PARTY WITH PIZZA AND A MOVIE

8. Encourage <u>self-evaluation</u>.

- Self-evaluation and self-criticism are different. Self-criticism holds a student hostage to the past:
  "I never do anything right."
- Self-evaluation can help the student <u>focus on improvement</u>:
  "Next time, I'm going to start my homework earlier."
- Suggest using self-evaluation <u>techniques</u>:
  "Am I satisfied with my paper? Did I use Spellcheck and carefully proofread the final draft?"
- Some students have a realistic view of their performance and can discuss it while others may be defensive. If feedback is warranted, be <u>positive first</u>; then point out the <u>specific concern</u>; finally, pose a <u>question</u> that will keep the student involved in the process:
  "You made some interesting points in your essay, but I had some trouble following it. What could you do to improve the flow of ideas?"

- If the student needs help, try to <u>model the thinking process</u>:

  Example A: *"Remember what multiplication means. It's really a form of addition. Let's try 3 x 4. I want to give 3 of your friends – Sarah, Matt, and Tamika – 4 stickers each. Let's make a picture of your 3 friends, wearing 4 stickers on each of their shirts. Now, let's count the stickers. Okay, there are 12 stickers in all. We can see that multiplying means adding groups of the same number of things. What if we give 4 of your friends 3 stickers each?"*

  Example B: *"We know that the organization of a paper depends upon the development of main ideas and details. First, let's see if the main ideas follow a logical sequence by reading the topic sentence of each paragraph. Can the order of main ideas be changed to improve the paper's flow? Let's also make sure that the details follow a logical sequence within each paragraph. I remember that an outline was helpful the last time you wrote an essay. Did you use one this time?"*

- When a student reflects on his own learning style and develops a way to approach a task, he is using a high level of <u>strategic planning</u>.

- <u>Reactions</u> to grades and teachers' comments require another kind of self-evaluation.

  If the student is defensive about a grade, try to <u>understand</u> his reaction and <u>validate</u> his feelings:
  "You must feel discouraged."

  Once the student begins to <u>discuss</u> his feelings, he may be able to assess the situation more objectively:
  "What grade would you have given yourself? What do you think the teacher expected?"

  The goal is for the student to <u>consider</u> the teacher's point of view, <u>learn</u> from the teacher's comments, and <u>apply</u> this information to future tasks.

  At the same time, it is important for students to become <u>independent thinkers</u>, able to approach a teacher with their own ideas.

  After practicing self-evaluation, students may have to move past a disappointment. This <u>coping skill</u> will benefit them throughout life.

9. Recommend an <u>attractive presentation</u>.

- When the student has completed the basic requirements of an assignment, encourage her to <u>show off</u> her work.

- Before one paragraph is read, before one math problem is corrected, before content is evaluated – the teacher observes the student's work.

- Suggest adding finishing touches when appropriate – a special <u>cover</u>, a <u>title page</u>, <u>illustrations</u>.

- An impressive presentation not only makes a difference to the teacher, it can heighten the student's appreciation of her own work.

10. Set up a <u>study group</u>.

- Introduce the student to the idea of starting or joining a study group.

- Explain the benefits of doing schoolwork within a small group:

  Students can achieve a greater understanding of subject matter – particularly if it is complicated – when they have the opportunity to <u>share</u>, <u>discuss</u>, and <u>compare</u> ideas.

  As students in a study group work together toward a <u>common goal</u>, they can help each other not only academically but also emotionally.

  Students can bring a <u>variety of strengths</u> to the group: a clear note-taking style, strong reading comprehension, good organizational skills.

When given the <u>opportunity to teach</u> or explain a concept to someone else, students enhance their own understanding.

Coming together as a group adds a <u>social component</u> to studying, increasing motivation and enabling more material to be covered.

- Use the following guidelines when planning a study group:

An ideal number is from <u>four to six students</u>.

Members must be <u>serious</u> about doing well in school. They should participate and take notes in class, do their homework, and want to study.

The group should meet in a place where the students can <u>spread out</u> and <u>concentrate</u>. Often libraries have study rooms for small groups.

The group should <u>meet regularly</u> (i.e., once a week) – on the same day and at the same time. For certain assignments or final exams, the group can schedule more meetings.

The group should meet for a maximum of <u>three hours</u>; one or two hours can be sufficient. When an ending time is specified, the students are more motivated to focus.

- Encourage the students to <u>structure</u> their study group for better results:

Choose a <u>group leader</u> who will outline the <u>objectives</u> and institute certain <u>routines</u>.

At the start of every session, assign a <u>volunteer moderator</u> who will keep the members on task.

Build in five- to ten-minute <u>breaks</u> for socializing and moving around, which will help keep members focused during study times.

Take turns covering a topic. <u>Teaching</u> a concept is a way to improve memory and understanding.

At the end of each session, spend a few minutes making <u>plans</u> for the next meeting, so students can be prepared.

- Help the students think of different ways to use the study group:

Review class <u>notes</u> together and clarify important points.

Coordinate notes from assigned reading with class notes.

Construct a <u>study guide</u> from combined notes.

Predict <u>test questions</u> and outline possible essay questions.

Come up with creative ways to study and learn together.

One student can prepare <u>notecards</u> with terms and definitions before the meeting, then test the rest of the students.

Another student can bring a list of possible essay questions for the group to discuss.

- The goal of a study group is to enhance memory and enrich learning. Students should agree to be respectful and allow everyone in the group to participate. They should not waste time arguing about procedure, changing the subject, or fooling around. The group leader should make sure that everyone remains <u>on task</u> and moving forward.

"I was just born disorganized. I can't help it."

Some simple strategies can help students save time and increase productivity. This section offers some tips on setting up an effective study environment.

1. Find places that are <u>conducive to learning</u>.

- Choose <u>work spaces</u> where the student can <u>focus</u>. These locations can vary according to individual needs and the kind of homework assigned. When preparing for a test, it can even be advantageous to vary study locations.

- A <u>desk</u> in a student's room is fine, but if the student uses a <u>computer</u>, perhaps locate it in a <u>common area</u> where it is easier to oversee.

- Younger students may work more productively at the <u>kitchen table</u>, which may provide a sense of <u>security</u> that heightens concentration.

- Sometimes, <u>contact</u> with the family or caregiver can be useful. Students can ask for <u>help</u>, and parents can <u>monitor</u> homework and computer use, if necessary.

- Working in a place that is <u>not perfectly quiet</u> can help students learn to tune out minor disturbances that may occur in other situations.

- For some students, <u>background</u> "noise," such as music, can reduce the stress of doing homework (provided they are not distracted by it).

- Doing homework on a bed, couch, or floor, while unconventional, is acceptable if the student can still be efficient.

- Students have to recognize that <u>different activities</u> require different <u>levels of attention</u>. Choose a space that is appropriate for the task. For example, writing a paper requires complex thinking, so work in a library or another quiet location.

- Some students are easily <u>distracted</u>, even by items in the work space. Analyze and minimize these disturbances.
See Samples A & B.

A: Investigating Distractions

WATCH THE STUDENT.
- During a homework session of about 20-30 minutes, <u>notice what disturbs</u> the student's focus.
- <u>Make a list</u> of the student's distractions.
- Ask the student to <u>name other distractions</u> and add them to the list.

ANALYZE THE DISTRACTION LIST.
- <u>Think of solutions</u>: specific actions that can help lessen or eliminate distractions.
- Encourage the student to come up with ideas, and <u>brainstorm together</u>.
- <u>Write down the actions</u> next to each distraction listed.

TAKE ACTION.
- Before beginning the next homework session, ask the student to <u>follow through</u> with the actions on the list.
- <u>Make a new list</u> of distractions.
- <u>Compare</u> the two lists.

CONSIDER THE RESULTS.
- Were there fewer distractions?
- Was there a greater degree of attention?
- What can the student conclude from this experiment?

B: Distraction-Action Example

DISTRACTIONS	ACTIONS
Tom complained about being hungry.	Eat a snack before starting homework or plan a snack break.
He needed an eraser.	Set up a work station with school supplies at hand.
He played with fun items on his desk.	Clear the desk of unnecessary, distracting items.
He answered his cell phone.	Turn off the cell phone during homework sessions.

2. Use this DISTRACTION-ACTION form to analyze behavior and improve focus.

- Watch the student and list <u>distractions</u> in the left column.
- Ask the student if there were any other distractions and add them to the list.
- Analyze the list and, for each distraction, brainstorm a <u>solution</u>.
- Next to each distraction, write an <u>action</u> that will prevent the interruption.
- Before and during the next homework session, <u>follow the actions</u> suggested.
- Repeat the experiment if necessary.

DISTRACTIONS	ACTIONS

DISTRACTIONS	ACTIONS

3. <u>Equip</u> a study area.

- Organize a <u>work space</u> at a desk or table, or, if it is necessary to move around, use a <u>container</u> to store equipment.

- Pay attention to <u>lighting</u>. The amount of light, position of lamps, and kind of lightbulbs can make an impact on the study environment. Reduce glare on the computer to relieve eye strain.

- Where to locate a <u>computer</u> is up to the family. Just remember that students use the Internet for socializing as well as schoolwork.

- Encourage students to select and organize their own <u>supplies</u>.
  See Sample C.

4. Establish a <u>filing system</u>.

- An organized filing system allows students to <u>archive important papers</u>, so they can be accessed easily for <u>research</u> or <u>review</u>. Students should clean out their backpacks regularly, file papers that may be useful later, and discard any excess.

- Label a <u>hanging file</u> for each subject: ENGLISH, HISTORY, SCIENCE, MATH, SPANISH, MUSIC.

- Label file <u>folders</u> with the following categories: Homework, Notes/Handouts, Tests/Quizzes, and Papers/Projects. Insert a set of folders into each hanging file.

- Use a file cabinet, drawer, or box for school files.

- Younger students can use a <u>stand-alone accordion file</u> to save important schoolwork.
  See Sample D.

Sample: Study Area

C: Checklist for Supplies

DATE BOOK OR ELECTRONIC ORGANIZER	PAPER CLIPS
MONTHLY CALENDAR	STAPLER AND STAPLES
——	STAPLE REMOVER
COMPUTER	HOLE PUNCHER
PRINTER/SCANNER	REINFORCEMENTS
FLASH DRIVE	ADHESIVE TAPES
BLANK CDs AND CASES	GLUE
MONITOR CLEANER	RULER
CALCULATOR	SCISSORS
——	PENCIL SHARPENER
PENS AND PENCILS	DICTIONARY
ERASERS	THESAURUS
WITE-OUT	DESK ENCYCLOPEDIA
COLORED MARKERS	ATLAS OR GLOBE
HIGHLIGHTERS	——
——	FILE DRAWER OR BOX
SPIRAL NOTEBOOKS	HANGING FILES
LOOSE-LEAF BINDERS	FILE FOLDERS
INDEX CARDS AND FILE BOXES	REPORT COVERS
——	——
LOOSE-LEAF PAPER	LABEL MAKER
GRAPH PAPER	BOOK STAND
PRINTER PAPER	TENSOR LAMP
COLORED PAPER	______________
PAGE SAVERS	______________
NOTEPADS	______________
POST-IT NOTES	______________

Sample: Filing System

D: Labeling

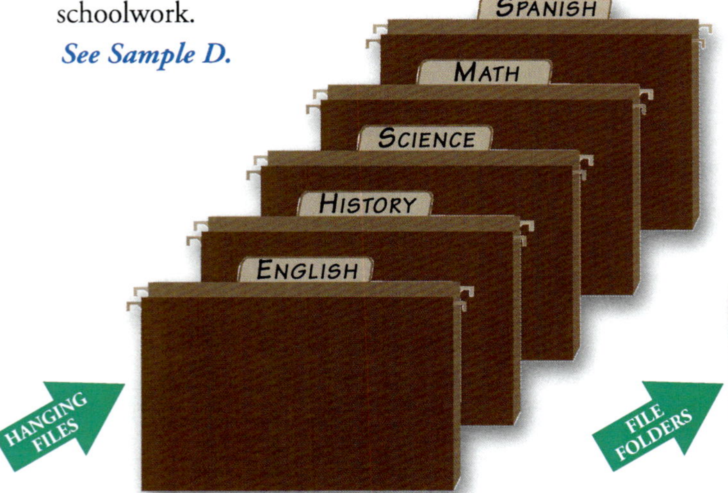

5. Try color coding.

- Choose <u>different colors</u> for different subjects.

- <u>Coordinate colors</u> of hanging files, file folders, loose-leaf binders, and spiral notebooks. Doing this can help the student distinguish between subjects and makes filing easier.

- If finding a variety of colors is difficult, purchase plain binders with see-through pockets, and slip in different pieces of <u>colored paper</u>. Otherwise, use <u>colored stickers</u>.

- Encourage students to <u>decorate binders</u> with illustrations pertaining to the subject. Personalizing school supplies can be a motivational tool.
  See Samples E & F.

6. Invest in a label maker.

- Labels that are <u>printed</u> help materials look more organized.

- A younger student can work a label maker with adult supervision (cartridges are expensive). An older student may appreciate owning one.

- Computer-generated labels are also an option, but they are not as simple to produce.

7. Schedule a time to file.

- Establish a time for filing – maybe at the end of each week or once a month and before vacations.

- Make it a <u>requirement</u> – perhaps part of an allowance chore.

- For many students, listening to <u>music</u> while filing can help make the task seem less tedious.

- Once the filing has been done a few times, it becomes easier. Affirm the <u>rewarding feeling</u>: "It must feel good to have a lighter backpack."

8. Set up a keepsake file.

- At the end of the school year, help the student <u>clean out</u> the regular files.

- Put keepsakes – <u>choice</u> pieces of work – and useful <u>reference</u> items in a box or drawer. <u>Label</u> by <u>grade</u>.
  See Sample G.

E: Color-Coded Hanging Files for Subjects

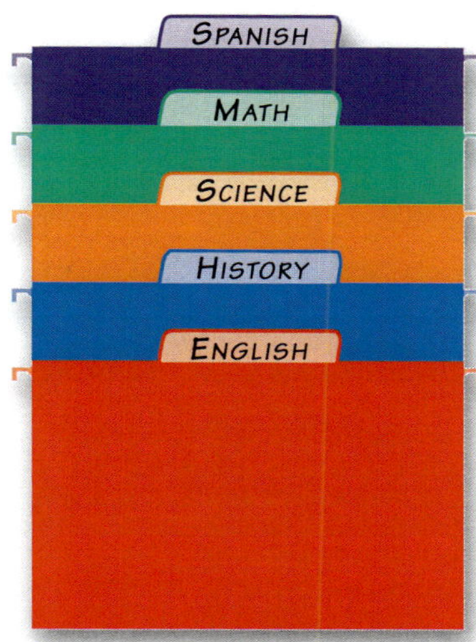

F: Color-Coordinated Materials by Subject
Hanging File with Folders

Loose-Leaf Binder Spiral Notebook

G: Files by Grade

* *Students can save <u>index card boxes</u> of vocabulary words for future use.*

> **"I don't have enough time to do what I need to do, let alone time for what I want to do."**

It is possible, at any age, to become overextended. Why not learn early on that setting limits and priorities is the first step toward effective time management? After that, practicing some simple management techniques and making them habitual will help.

1. Use a <u>date book</u> for homework assignments.

- <u>Write</u> down homework assignments in a date book, such as a weekly planner.

- Hand-held <u>electronic devices</u> can work with planners but not necessarily replace them. Teachers often restrict the use of pdas (personal digital assistants) or smart phones during the school day.

- When students bring a <u>laptop</u> to class, they can use calendar or scheduler software, but a small date book is easier to handle.

- If teachers provide <u>assignment sheets</u>, transfer the homework and due dates into the planner. Store the assignment sheets in their respective subject notebooks or folders.

- Establishing the routine of recording assignments in one place can help students <u>plan</u> their homework and <u>manage</u> their time effectively:

  "I have a quiz on Wednesday in math, so I'm going to read ahead in Animal Farm. *Then I can study more for math on Tuesday."*

  "My poster is due on Friday. I'm going to start it on Monday and schedule time every day until it's done."

- To quickly recall school subjects, make up an acronym: H.E.L.M.S. for <u>H</u>ISTORY, <u>E</u>NGLISH, <u>L</u>ATIN, <u>M</u>ATH, <u>S</u>CIENCE.

- Develop <u>shorthand</u> methods for copying down assignments. For example, p. for page (pp. for pages), ch. for chapter, AF for *Animal Farm*.

- In addition to recording homework assignments, jot down important <u>personal notes</u> and after-school <u>activities</u>.

- <u>Carry</u> the date book back and forth between home and school.
  See Sample A.

Sample: Date Book

A: Homework Assignments

20-22	APRIL
HISTORY, ENGLISH, LATIN, MATH, SCIENCE	
20 MON	
	H: JFK – Note Cards DUE TOMORROW
	E: Animal Farm – pp. 15-28
	L: Translation 7a
Bake Sale $	M: p. 165, 1-11 (odd #s)
	S: Poster – research
	Flute – 4pm
21 TUE	
	H: JFK – Intro/Thesis
	E: AF – pp. 29-41
	L: Translation 7b
Mindy's Birthday Yay!	M: Ch. 15 – QUIZ TOMORROW
	S: Poster – pics. Snacks for Meeting
22 WED	
	H: JFK – Intro/Thesis
	E: AF – Write reflection
	L: p. 44, 1-10
GAME 5:30 Home	M: NO HOMEWORK
	S: Write up lab report/Poster – captions
	DUE TOMORROW

23-26	APRIL
HISTORY, ENGLISH, LATIN, MATH, SCIENCE	
23 THU	
	H: JFK – Intro/Thesis DUE TOMORROW
	E: Vocab. – sheet 12
Student Council (LUNCH)	L: Quiz TOMORROW (see sheet)
	M: p. 168, 1-10
	S: NO HOMEWORK
24 FRI	
	H: Newspaper article on CT Primary
	E: AF – pp. 42-70
Mindy's PARTY 8PM	L: p. 52, 1-20
	M: p. 172, 1-13 (odd) & π Day Ideas
	S: Txtbk. pp. 165-170, wkbk. p. 54

2. Use a monthly calendar as an overview.

- Display a monthly calendar at home: wall hanging, blotter, notebook.
- Write down the due dates of long-term assignments, such as papers, projects, and tests.
- Incorporate significant after-school activities and vacation times.
- Check the monthly calendar regularly to plan ahead:

  "May is a very busy month. In addition to regular activities and daily homework, a history research paper is due on Friday, May 17; an English essay is due after the long weekend; and a math final is scheduled at the end of the month."

- Students must be aware of future engagements, so they can plan well in advance and integrate long-term assignments into their daily schedules.
  See Sample B.

B: Long-Term Assignments

APRIL

| Sunday | Monday | Tuesday | Wednesday | Thursday | Friday | Saturday |

MAY

Sunday	Monday	Tuesday	Wednesday	Thursday	Friday	Saturday
			1	2	3 Sarah's SLEEPOVER 7PM	4 Brian's BAR MITZVAH 10AM
5	6 HISTORY Research Paper JFK – 1st Draft	7	8 GAME – away	9	10	11
12 (MOTHER'S DAY) BOTANICAL GARDENS	13	14	15 GAME – home	16	17 HISTORY Research Paper JFK – FINAL DRAFT	18 DANCE – 8PM
19	20	21	22 GAME – home	23	24	25 VACATION Cooperstown
26	27 MEMORIAL DAY (OBSERVED)	28 ENGLISH Essay Animal Farm	29	30 MATH FINAL	31	

3. Break down <u>long-term assignments</u>.

- <u>Divide</u> a long-term assignment into separate tasks.

- <u>Estimate</u> the time needed for each task.

- <u>Schedule</u> periods during the week to work on individual tasks, and write them in the weekly planner.

- Use a <u>different color</u> ink for long-term assignments, so they stand out.

- Set aside larger <u>blocks of time</u> on the <u>weekends</u> to work on long-term assignments. The week feels so much more manageable if some time is taken during the weekend to <u>get ahead</u>.

- If the teacher provides a <u>time line</u> for completing an assignment, transfer the individual <u>due dates</u> into the weekly planner.
  See Sample C.

4. Learn to use <u>study time</u> effectively.

- Students may underestimate or even overestimate the time they need to finish their homework, which can cause unnecessary stress.

- Here is a tactic that will help students <u>plan</u> their time and <u>focus</u> while they work:

  Ask them to look over the homework assignments for the day and <u>estimate</u> the time it will take to complete each one.

  <u>Jot down</u> the estimated numbers (Language Arts – 20 minutes, Science – 45 minutes, and so on).

  Set a <u>timer</u> before the student begins each assignment, and record the results.

  Check to see whether the homework is completed within the time allotted, to the student's satisfaction, and at a high level.

- Try this routine more than once, making adjustments, until the student is able to <u>evaluate</u> the time needed to finish homework assignments. This tactic also helps the student pay <u>close attention</u> to the task at hand.

Sample: Long-Term Assignments

C: Separate Tasks (For Research Paper)

BACKGROUND INFORMATION
Check a desk encyclopedia or search an Internet site for a summary of the subject.

SOURCES
Investigate sources in the library and on the Internet.

BIBLIOGRAPHY
Create source note cards that will be the basis of a bibliography.

THESIS STATEMENT
Develop a thesis for the paper that will guide the research.

OUTLINE
Construct an outline. Include an introduction and a conclusion. Jot down page numbers in the margins to relocate information later.

NOTE CARDS
Take plenty of notes. This information makes up the paper's content. Organize note cards to coincide with the outline.

FIRST DRAFT
Begin the writing process. Include an introductory paragraph, body paragraphs, and a conclusion.

REVISE AND EDIT
Check content, organization, language, and mechanics.

FINAL DRAFT
Proofread and Spellcheck.

FINAL BIBLIOGRAPHY
Include sources that were used for the paper. Copy information from the source cards. Make sure the format is correct.

5. Choose <u>after-school activities</u> carefully.

- Think about what <u>energizes</u> the student. Build on this energy.

- Weigh the <u>investment</u>. If all other things are equal, which activity better transfers into later life?

- Find an activity that the student both <u>enjoys</u> and <u>does well</u>. This combination is a winner. It can strengthen self-esteem and lead to a long-term commitment.

- Encouraging the student to participate in an activity that is considered <u>important by parents or teachers</u> may be beneficial or even necessary.

  For example, a parent may want the student to participate in sports to get more exercise, or a teacher may recommend that a student receive extra help in a particular subject.

- Whatever the circumstances, life is a balancing act for adults and children alike. Involve students in the process of <u>prioritizing</u>:

  NECESSARY ACTIVITIES (eating, sleeping, exercising)

  FAMILY RESPONSIBILITIES (visiting Grandma, doing chores, attending religious services)

  SCHOOLWORK (being attentive in class, organizing materials, doing homework at a high level)

  WORTHWHILE ACTIVITIES (sports, music, community service)

  DOWN TIME (being with friends, watching TV, playing games)

- Suggest that students view school as their <u>job</u>. After Necessary Activities and Family Responsibilities, Schoolwork comes first.

6. Evaluate <u>time</u> for after-school activities.

- Saying yes to worthwhile activities is easy, but try not to overcommit.

- Make an <u>hourly grid</u> of the student's after-school activities.

- Fill in the time spent participating in these activities – sports, music lessons, jobs – and include <u>travel</u> times.

- Remember to insert times for <u>dinner</u>.

- Take a look at the results. Does the student have enough time to do <u>homework</u> at a high level? Is there time to eat dinner together as a family? Is there enough time for the student to get a good night's <u>sleep</u>?

  See Samples D & E.

D: Overcommitted Schedule

	MON	TUE	WED	THU	FRI
3 PM	soccer	soccer	soccer	soccer	yearbook
4 PM	↓	↓	↓	↓	↓
5 PM	math tutor	guitar practice	**homework**	guitar practice	girl scouts
6 PM	dinner	dinner	youth group	cooking class	
7 PM	guitar lesson	band practice	dinner	dinner	dinner
8 PM	**homework**		babysitting	**homework**	☺
9 PM	↓	↓	↓	↓	↓

☺ = free time

E: More Balanced Schedule

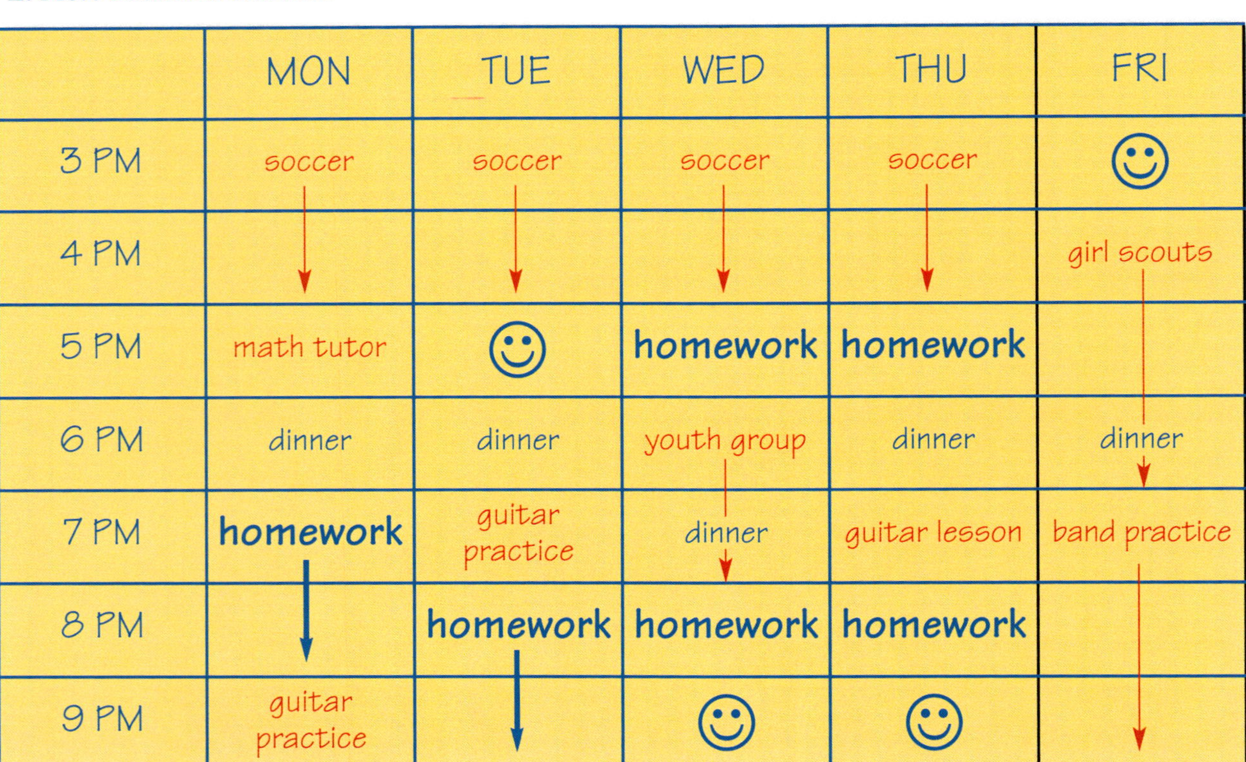

	MON	TUE	WED	THU	FRI
3 PM	soccer	soccer	soccer	soccer	☺
4 PM	↓	↓	↓	↓	girl scouts
5 PM	math tutor	☺	**homework**	**homework**	
6 PM	dinner	dinner	youth group	dinner	dinner
7 PM	**homework**	guitar practice	dinner	guitar lesson	band practice
8 PM	↓	**homework**	**homework**	**homework**	
9 PM	guitar practice	↓	☺	☺	↓

7. Make the <u>weekend</u> productive.

- There are enough hours in a weekend to enjoy extracurricular activities, social engagements, and downtime, while still scheduling periods for <u>homework</u> and <u>long-term assignments</u>.

- There are at least <u>36 waking hours</u> during the course of a weekend. If a high school student has three to four hours of homework, more than 90% of the weekend is left for other activities.

- Try an experiment: Make up an <u>hourly grid</u> for the weekend starting with Friday. Fill in the spaces with required activities, including sports, family obligations, and social engagements. How much time is left over? There should be plenty of time for schoolwork and relaxation, too.

- If, on the other hand, students do not have sufficient time on the weekends to do homework at a high level, catch up with organizational tasks, get a handle on long-term assignments, and relax, then they may be overbooked. Occasionally, it may be unavoidable, but it should not become a pattern. Try to protect the student's weekends.

- Encourage the student to make conscious <u>choices</u> about when to do schoolwork on the weekend. Here are some options:

  Complete homework on <u>Friday</u>, so the rest of the weekend is free.

  Do homework in <u>increments</u> throughout the weekend, in between other activities, so it feels less overwhelming.

  Wait until <u>Sunday</u> to begin homework, as long as there is not too much. Then the material will be fresh for Monday. However, avoid beginning too late, which can be stressful and start the week out badly.

- Doing assignments <u>in advance</u> of their due dates can be remarkably satisfying. Consider using the weekend and vacations to get ahead.
  See Sample F.

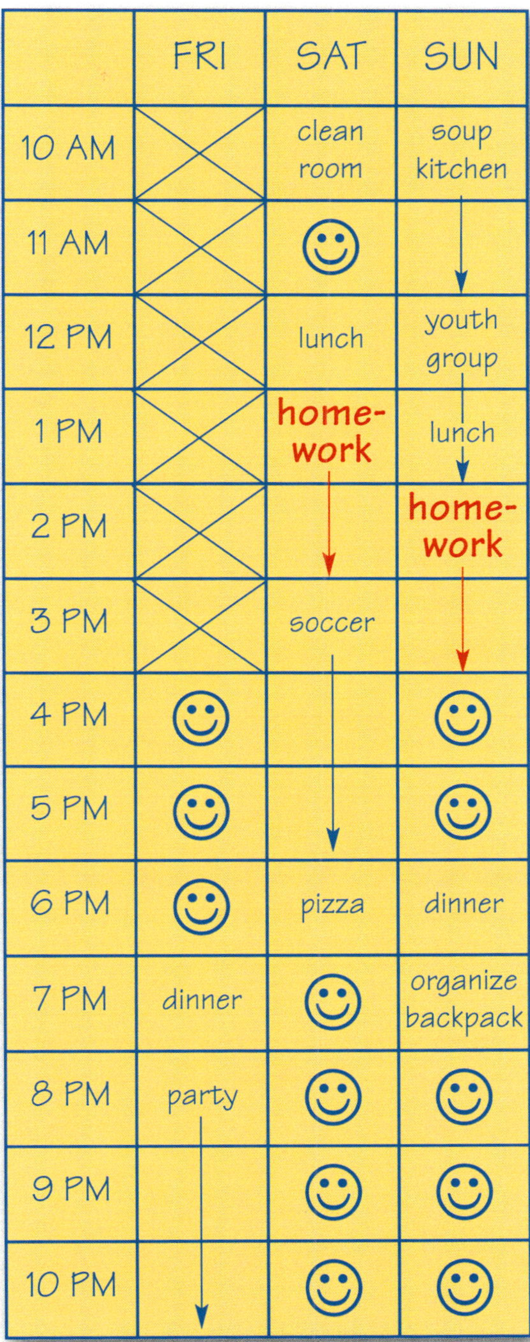

Sample: Weekend Schedule

F: Hourly Grid

	FRI	SAT	SUN
10 AM		clean room	soup kitchen
11 AM		☺	
12 PM		lunch	youth group
1 PM		home-work	lunch
2 PM			home-work
3 PM		soccer	
4 PM	☺		☺
5 PM	☺		☺
6 PM	☺	pizza	dinner
7 PM	dinner	☺	organize backpack
8 PM	party	☺	☺
9 PM		☺	☺
10 PM		☺	☺

☺ = free time

> **"I'm a good reader, so why do I have trouble understanding what I read?"**

Recognizing words is only the first step. Reading requires comprehension – understanding text. Whether reading a primer or a college textbook, the approaches are similar. Use the strategies in this section to learn how to grasp and retain the content of reading material.

1. Preview content.

- There are various reasons to preview the content of reading material – to find the appropriate reading level, to choose an interesting book, to locate information.

- For pleasure reading – perhaps a novel or chapter book for the young reader – read the back cover or dust jacket for a summary or review.

- For a more in-depth preview of textbooks, reference books, technical material, journal articles, or electronic sources, read tables of contents, chapter names, topics, subtopics, and headings, and skim the text.

2. Obtain background information.

- Before beginning to read, the student may need background information.

- If the student does not understand the reading, it could simply mean that the subject matter is unfamiliar.

- For younger students, fill in the blanks when necessary. Use descriptions, visual aids, references, and real-life experiences, but be careful not to overload them with too many details.

- Encourage older students to acquire background information. They should learn to implement this strategy on their own.

- Have on hand a dictionary or small, one-volume desk encyclopedia to look up brief descriptions of people, places, terms, and concepts. Search for information online: Wikipedia provides a quick overview of a subject.

See Samples A, B, & C.

Samples: Background Information

A: Description

The novel takes place during the Civil War.

The student may need a reminder that this was an internal war between the northern and southern states, in part over the issue of slavery.

B: Visual Aid

The story is set in an African village.

Use a map or globe.

"Can you find Africa?"

Explain that Africa is a large continent with lots of countries.

"Do you know what a continent is?"

Find the general location of the village in which the story is set.

"Can you say the name of this country?

Briefly describe what the area is like as it pertains to the story.

C: Reference

The article is about egrets.

Have the student look up the word *egret* to find a concise description – in a dictionary, desk encyclopedia, or online.

Reading Comprehension

3. Read with a purpose.

- Presenting <u>objectives</u> for reading helps to spark interest, sustain attention, and enhance comprehension.

- For the younger student, create a purpose for reading:

  "Read this sentence to find out why Maria thinks Johnny is funny."

  "Read this chapter to learn why the seasons change."

  "What does the title of this book mean to you?"

- An <u>assignment</u> provides a purpose for reading. For example, students are asked to answer questions, write essays, or review material for tests.

4. Determine <u>main ideas</u>.

- Once the content is previewed, the background information obtained, and the purpose identified, begin to read.

- Look for the main ideas. They provide anchors for comprehension.

- A main idea can be defined as a <u>broad concept</u>, <u>central theme</u>, or <u>category</u> that incorporates smaller facts and ideas.

- The human mind seeks <u>order</u>. Forming categories of information is an essential part of the thinking process. The mind automatically makes room for new information as it enters a category.

- Remember, there are <u>levels</u> of main ideas: A title is broader than a chapter name, which is broader than the topic sentence, which contains the main idea of a paragraph.

- Find main ideas in <u>titles</u>, <u>subtitles</u>, <u>prefaces</u>, <u>tables of contents</u>, <u>introductions</u>, <u>chapter names</u>, <u>topics</u>, <u>subtopics</u>, <u>headings</u>, <u>summaries</u>, and <u>topic sentences</u> of paragraphs. (A topic sentence is often the first sentence of a paragraph but not always.)

- Main ideas can be <u>stated or implied</u>. If implied, inferential thinking will be necessary.
  (For more about inferential thinking: Step 6)
  See Samples D, E, F, & G.

D: Primary Reader

Norma Jean liked to jump.

In the morning she jumped out of bed.

She jumped into her clothes.

She jumped down the stairs.

Norma Jean jumped all the way to school.

She jumped past Amy, Sam, Nell, and Ted.

"Wow!" said Ted. "Look at her go!

That Norma Jean never stops jumping!"

— Joanna Cole, *Norma Jean, Jumping Bean*

E: Textbook

To a scientist, <u>work</u> means using a *force* to move an *object* through a *distance*. Thus, work is related to motion. In everyday language we might say that sitting at a desk reading this book is "work." But in a scientific sense, we could not call this work. In order for work to be done, some object must be moved through a distance.

— Earl S. Morrison, Alan Moore, Nan Armour, Allan Hammond, John Haysom, Elinor Nicoll, and Muriel Smyth, *Scienceplus: Technology and Society*

F: Chapter Book

She sighed and moved on to the other cupboard, this one a jumble of huge sea shells, pink, violet, bone-white. They looked, she thought, with their open ends toward her, as if they were all humming with the sound of the sea, which she knew she would hear if she opened the cupboard door, took one out and held it to her ear. She wondered if the humming of so many shells would fill the room if she were to open the door.

— Norma Kassirer, *Magic Elizabeth*

5. Identify details.

- The essence of a subject emerges through the development of detailed information.

- Look for the details. They are the smaller facts and ideas that can be considered the components of a main idea. They can be stated or implied.

- Details support a main idea. If the main idea of a paragraph is stated in the first sentence, then the details follow it. Otherwise, the details may surround or lead up to the main idea. Remember, the sentence that contains the main idea of a paragraph is the topic sentence.

- Details are also found in illustrations – charts, graphs, maps, pictures, tables.

- Connect the details to their corresponding main ideas. This is the ongoing process by which content is understood and becomes more automatic as reading skills develop.

- Connecting details to their main ideas is also the primary strategy for note taking, studying, and writing.

  See Samples D, E, F, & G.

6. Use literal and inferential thinking.

- Reading is a kind of thinking.

- Literal thinking, while reading, involves the comprehension of facts and ideas that are directly stated in the text.

- Inferential thinking, while reading, involves the evolution of new ideas by drawing conclusions – in other words, "reading between the lines."

- The process of making inferences is as follows:

  Students extract information from the text.

  The information is added to their fund of knowledge on the subject.

  They put it all together and draw a conclusion.

- Predicting outcomes – thinking about what is going to happen next – is an integral part of the reading process and a kind of inferential thinking. It is a skill that can help keep students interested in the reading material.

G: Nonfiction

What are we to do, adrift in a sea of ignorance? Some are nihilistic and say, "Nothing." They propose only that we should continue to drift, as if no course could possibly be charted in such a vast sea which would bring us to any true clarity or meaningful destination. But others, sufficiently aware to know that they are lost, dare to hope that they can work themselves out of ignorance through developing even greater awareness. They are correct. It is possible. But such greater awareness does not come to them in a single blinding flash of enlightenment. It comes slowly, piece by piece, and each piece must be worked for by the patient effort of study and observation of everything, including themselves. They are humble students. **The path of spiritual growth is a path of lifelong learning.**

– M. Scott Peck, M.D., *The Road Less Traveled*

Samples: Literal & Inferential Thinking

H: Modeling the Thinking Process

TEXT: The air at the top of Mount Everest is extremely thin.

QUESTION: How might this fact influence a mountain climber?

KNOWLEDGE: Air contains oxygen, and people need oxygen to survive.

INFERENCE: A mountain climber will need to carry oxygen when climbing Mount Everest.

I: Primary Reader

TEXT: Hi. My name is Harry. I live with my family in this cave. My friends like to run and jump and swing and climb. I like those things too. But most of all I like to make new things. Things no one has ever seen before.

INFERENCE: While looking at the illustrations and reading that Harry lives in a cave with his family, the student can infer that this is a story about early man and can predict what a boy might invent.

– Cathy East Dubowski and Mark Dubowski, *Cave Boy*

- For younger students, ask a question that can lead to a prediction:

  "What do you think is in the box?"

  "Maybe it's Margaret's missing bracelet."

- Keep in mind, literal comprehension is the first step. <u>Stated facts</u> and ideas must be understood if they are to be drawn upon to make inferences. ***See Samples H, I, & J.***

7. Use <u>critical reading</u> skills.

- Critical reading involves <u>analyzing</u> and <u>assimilating</u> (putting together) pieces of information.

- Read with an inquiring mind, interpret reading material, and form a <u>point of view</u>.

- Here are some examples of applying critical reading skills:

  <u>Integrate</u> information from several sources for a research paper.

  <u>Determine</u> why a character in literature behaves in a particular way.

  <u>Compare</u> two scientists' theories.

- An assignment often requires students to justify their analysis. Be prepared to explain an interpretation by using <u>examples</u> from the reading.

- The critical reading process may involve <u>rereading</u> and <u>pondering</u>, especially with difficult material. ***See Sample K.***

8. Find <u>meanings</u> for unknown words.

- While reading, keep a <u>dictionary</u> close by. Establish the habit of looking up unknown words. Learning new words has the added benefit of broadening <u>vocabulary</u>.

- Sometimes, for a younger student, supplying the <u>meaning</u> of a word prevents interruption of concentration.

- Use <u>context clues</u> to help recognize and define words. Context in reading refers to the facts and ideas that surround a word and can reveal its meaning.

J: Textbook

TEXT: All living things are part of a complex network of interactions called the web of life. Much as the strands of silk in a spider's web bind one segment to another, feeding and other interactions bind all organisms to one another. Like other animals, humans form a part of the web of life. Frequently we forget our connections to the other organisms that inhabit the earth. We are reminded of them, however, whenever our actions have visible effects on our surroundings.

INFERENCE: In this text, the comparison between a spider's web and the connection of all organisms is directly stated. On the other hand, the reference to "feeding" <u>suggests</u> the principle of the food chain, and the statement "our actions have visible effects on our surroundings" <u>brings to mind</u> the destruction of our planet's natural habitats.

BSCS: A Science Education Curriculum Study, *Biological Science: An Ecological Approach*

Sample: Critical Reading

K: Speech

Text: It may be objected, however, that this pressing of the Negro's right to suffrage is premature. Let us have slavery abolished, it may be said, let us have labor organized, and then, in the natural course of events, the right of suffrage will be extended to the Negro. I do not agree with this. The constitution of the human mind is such, that if it once disregards the conviction forced upon it by a revelation of truth, it requires the exercise of a higher power to produce the same conviction afterward.

Assignment: Explain Douglass' argument that an African-American's right to vote must be enacted at the same time as the abolition of slavery.

Explanation: According to Douglass, if one does not act on a conviction immediately, the power of that conviction will be lost. It seems he believed that if the right to vote was not provided at the same time as the freeing of slaves, it could be forgotten or considered less important at a later date.

– Frederick Douglass, "What the Black Man Wants"

- If a word does not seem essential to the meaning of the text, perhaps let it go. Sometimes, maintaining <u>concentration</u> can be more beneficial than defining a word.

- Realize that authors of textbooks often plant new words purposely as part of a lesson, but if more than a few words are unknown on one page, the <u>reading level</u> may be too high. *See Samples L & M.*

9. <u>Break down text</u> into manageable units.

- If a reading assignment is difficult, break it down into <u>smaller parts</u>.

- The goal is to <u>absorb one part</u> of the reading before moving on.

- Younger students may need guidance to check comprehension <u>sentence-by-sentence</u>. Even older students may have to break down reading material sentence-by-sentence when the text is technical or especially dense.

- At other times, checking for comprehension <u>paragraph-by-paragraph</u> may be appropriate.

- The length of a manageable unit depends on the skill of the reader and the content.

10. <u>Reread</u> when necessary.

- Rereading is probably the most common method for absorbing challenging material.

- Remind students that it is acceptable to reread – even several times – when the material is confusing.

- In addition to rereading, <u>visualizing</u> and <u>verbalizing</u> the passage can be helpful.

  For example, a section in a science textbook that describes a complicated experiment could be made clear by picturing the steps while thinking or speaking them out loud.

- If troubleshooting strategies must be used often for the student to understand, then the reading level may be too high.

Samples: Meanings for Unknown Words

L: Context Clues – Primary Reader

TEXT: Some dinosaurs had ways to keep safe from Tyrannosaurus Rex. This dinosaur had hard plates on its back. The plates were like <u>armor</u>. When danger was near, it just sat tight.

FACTS SURROUNDING "ARMOR":

– hard plates on its back

– when danger was near, it just sat tight

MEANING FROM CONTEXT: From the clues given, the student can imagine pieces of a hard substance coming together to form a protective whole like a coat of <u>armor</u>.

– Joyce Milton, *Dinosaur Days*

M: Context Clues – Essay

TEXT: When first I took up my abode in the woods, that is, began to spend my nights as well as days there, which, by accident, was on Independence Day, or the fourth of July, 1845, my house was not finished for winter, but was merely a defense against the rain, without plastering or chimney, the walls being of rough weather-stained boards, with wide <u>chinks</u>, which made it cool at night.

FACTS SURROUNDING "CHINKS":

– an unfinished house

– no plaster

– walls of weather-stained boards

– wide chinks, making it cool at night

MEANING FROM CONTEXT: From the clues given, a <u>chink</u> seems to be some kind of opening.

– Henry David Thoreau, *Walden*

11. <u>Highlight</u> important information.

- Highlighting can <u>focus</u> attention and help the student <u>remember</u> information. It also enables the student to <u>review</u> the material at a later time.

- Highlight single words or phrases that will <u>trigger the memory</u> of complete facts and ideas. In some cases, full sentences may have to be highlighted.

- Highlighting involves making <u>choices</u> that depend on the assignment and needs of the student. For example, a student with less background information than another may have to highlight more.

- Remember, too much highlighting defeats the purpose: <u>emphasizing</u> specific material. It takes effort and practice to highlight enough but not too much.
  See Sample N.

N: Social Studies Textbook

BENJAMIN FRANKLIN

The greatest American of the Enlightenment was Benjamin Franklin. The story of his life begins in Boston, where he was born in 1706. His father was a soap and candle maker. Benjamin was the fifteenth of 17 children. He had only two years of schooling. At ten he became an apprentice in his father's shop, but after two years he shifted to the printer's trade, working for one of his nine older brothers.

When he was 17, Benjamin left Boston to seek his fortune in Philadelphia. Soon he owned his own printing shop, then also a newspaper, the *Pennsylvania Gazette*. He published books and wrote the annual *Poor Richard's Almanack*, each volume full of practical advice, weather predictions, odd bits of information, and what he called "scraps from the table of wisdom." One of the best-known examples of these "scraps" was the slogan "Early to bed, and early to rise, makes a man healthy, wealthy, and wise." Other typical examples are "God helps them that help themselves," "One today is worth two tomorrows," and "When the well is dry, they know the worth of water." He was so successful that by the time he was 42 he had enough money to live comfortably for the rest of his life.

At this point Franklin retired from the printing business so that he could pursue his other interests. These were almost endless. He invented a cast-iron fireplace (the Franklin stove), which radiated most of its heat into the room instead of allowing it to escape up the chimney. He invented bifocal eyeglasses so that people who were both nearsighted and farsighted need have only one pair. His famous experiment with a kite in a thunderstorm proved his theory that lightning was a form of electricity. This alone made his reputation among the leading European scientists of the time.

In addition to his scientific discoveries, Franklin was an outstanding citizen and public servant. He helped found the first library in Philadelphia, and the first fire department, and the first hospital, and a school – the Academy for the Education of Youth, which became the University of Pennsylvania...

– John A. Garraty, *The Story of America*

Reading Comprehension

12. <u>Take notes</u> while reading.

- Taking notes can heighten comprehension and help students prepare for classes, tests, and papers.

- Note taking condenses information into an informal outline format. It can <u>focus</u> attention, <u>clarify</u> content, and improve <u>recall</u>.

- Remember to <u>preview</u> the assigned reading for background information and to get a sense of its organization. Look at headings, subheadings, and dust jackets.

- Before beginning to take notes, read through <u>one section</u> of material to gain a basic under-standing of the content – one paragraph or a series of paragraphs under a heading, for example.

- Then go back and take notes by alternating between <u>reading</u>, <u>understanding</u>, <u>deciding</u> what is important, and <u>writing</u>.

- Label the notes with a <u>heading</u> that includes the name, date, subject, source, page range, and topic.

- Determine the first <u>main idea</u> – Remember, it may be stated or implied.

- Write the first main idea next to the left margin and <u>underline</u> it.

- Next write the corresponding <u>details</u> under the main idea. <u>Indent</u> and set off each detail with a <u>dash</u>.

- Break down information further by indenting again and inserting dashes.

- Continue to list main ideas and details in the same format.

- Write just enough to understand the notes when reading them later. Use <u>single words</u>, <u>phrases</u>, and <u>abbreviations</u> where possible.

- Students can organize details in <u>narrative</u> order – as the information unfolds in the reading or <u>chronological</u> order – as the information unfolds in date and time sequence.

- In all cases, when students <u>rewrite notes</u> they can revise the organization to suit the subject or assignment.
  See Sample O.

Reading Comprehension

13. Use an <u>assignment as a guide</u> for reading.

- Be sure to know the assignment before reading the text.

- Keep the assignment in mind while reading to <u>find</u>, <u>focus</u> on, and <u>comprehend</u> the relevant information.

- If there are <u>assignment questions</u>, read them before reading the text.

- Sometimes <u>scanning</u> material for specific information is appropriate – finding content for a paper or answering questions on a take-home test, for example.

14. Read <u>directions</u> carefully.

- Students sometimes glance through directions or skip them entirely, presuming they know what to do.

- Always read directions <u>carefully</u> and <u>completely</u>. Otherwise, students may provide the right answer to the wrong question.

- Directions often have several steps. Read through them to grasp the <u>basic content</u>. Then go back and <u>reread</u> them step by step, making sure each one is understood before moving on.

- If possible, <u>mark</u> the directions, so the main points are highlighted. Circle or underline <u>key words and phrases</u> to increase understanding and for easy reference.

- Avoid jumping to conclusions. This is one situation that requires the student to read and think <u>literally</u>, carefully following the specific directions.

See Samples P & Q.

> **"I have to take good notes, but I either take too many or not enough."**

Taking good notes involves recognizing important information and recording it in a concise and clear format. This section offers strategies for effective note taking.

ARRANGING NOTES

1. Organize a notebook.

- Various supplies can keep schoolwork organized: loose-leaf (three-ring) binders, spiral notebooks, folders.

- The <u>loose-leaf binder</u> provides maximal flexibility because material can be added and removed as needed. Younger students can include several or all of their subjects in one binder, while older students may want to use individual binders for each subject.

- Think about the <u>amount of material</u> that each subject is likely to produce before selecting the binder size. For example, a history class that meets daily is going to produce more material than a health class that meets once a week.

- Organize a subject according to the teacher's specifications. An English teacher may ask the students to divide the subject into skill areas: grammar, vocabulary, reading.

- If no system is provided, use one of the following:

  <u>Divide</u> a subject into sections that contain different kinds of schoolwork: Homework, Notes/Handouts, Tests/Quizzes, Papers/Projects. Within each section, order schoolwork by date.

  <u>Integrate</u> all types of schoolwork within a subject by date, eliminating the need for sections.

- Get into the habit of <u>labeling</u> every piece of schoolwork (homework, tests, handouts) with at least a name, date, and subject.
  See Samples A, B, & C.

A: Subject Divided into Sections

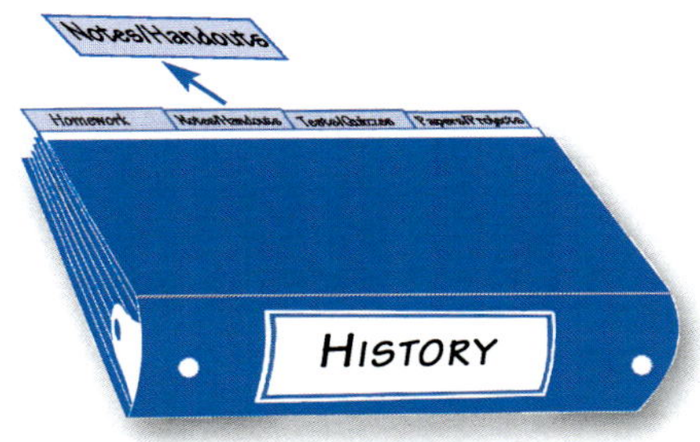

B: One Section of a Subject
(ordered by date)

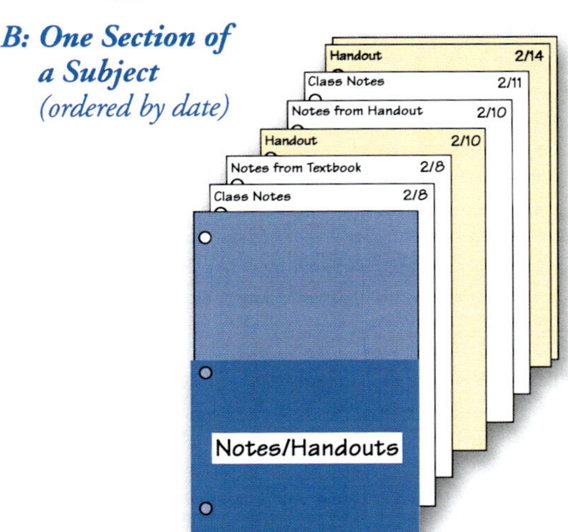

C: Subject Integrated
(ordered by date)

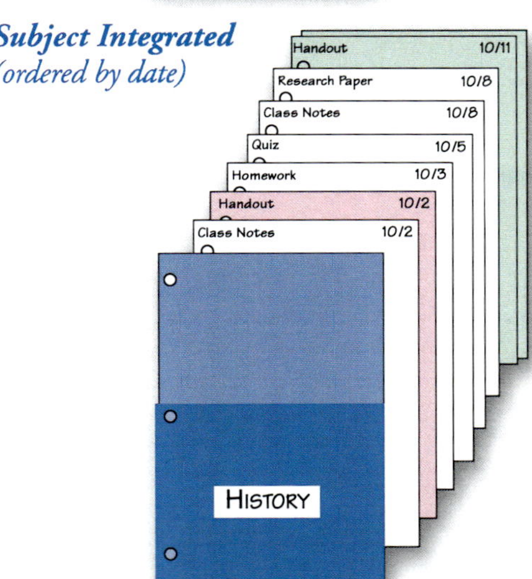

Note Taking

2. Use an **outline format**.

- An outline organizes <u>categories</u> of main ideas and supporting details.

- An <u>informal</u> outline is easy to prepare and ideal for taking notes in class or from reading material. Information is set off by indenting and using dashes.

- A <u>formal</u> outline involves a more systematic approach. It is often used when working on a comprehensive writing assignment. Information is set off by indenting and using Roman numerals (I, II, III), capital letters (A, B, C), Arabic numbers (1, 2, 3), and lower-case letters (a, b, c).

- A teacher may require students to take notes using a formal outline just to practice this skill.

- Writing notes in an <u>orderly</u> manner with <u>space</u> around items helps the student see the information more clearly and allows for adding notes later.

- <u>Word-processing</u> software provides automatic outline options with bullets or numbers.
  See Samples D & E.

NOTES FROM READING MATERIAL

3. Identify the **purpose** for note taking.

- The nature of an <u>assignment</u> determines the content of the notes.

  Reading a handout for a <u>class discussion</u>, for example, may involve jotting down some <u>interesting points</u>.

  An assignment to read a history chapter that will be included on a <u>test</u> requires <u>in-depth</u> note taking.

- While reading <u>literary works</u> (novels, plays, poems) to write an essay, students may base notes on <u>analysis</u> and interpretation. For test preparation, they may take <u>factual</u> notes on characters, settings, plot development, etc.

- When taking notes for a <u>research paper</u>, the student investigates a topic from a variety of <u>source materials</u> and coordinates the information.

  Take notes on <u>index cards</u>, so they can be easily classified and ordered.

- In all cases, it takes practice to record only notes that are <u>relevant to the assignment</u>.

Samples: Outline Format

D: Informal Outline

```
Name                          Social Studies
Date                             Class Notes
                                   (rewritten)
         HISTORY OF CIVILIZATION

Civilization – advanced level of culture

   - organized government

   - organized religion

   - division of labor

   - class structure

   - system of writing

Birthplace of 4 great civilizations

   - started in river valleys of Africa & Asia

      - Mesopotamia (1st) – between Tigris
        & Euphrates

      - Egypt – Nile

      - India – Indus

      - China – Yellow

   - rivers

      - water – drinking, cleaning, irrigation, etc.

      - irrigation – farming

      - fertile soil – farming

      - travel – trade
```

E: Formal Outline

```
Name                          Social Studies
Date                             Class Notes
                                   (rewritten)
         HISTORY OF CIVILIZATION

   I.  Civilization – advanced level of culture

       A. Organized government

       B. Organized religion

       C. Division of labor

       D. Class structure

       E. System of writing

  II.  Birthplace of 4 great civilizations

       A.  River valleys of Africa and Asia

           1. Mesopotamia (1st) – between Tigris
              and Euphrates

           2. Egypt – Nile

           3. India –  Indus

           4. China – Yellow

       B.  Rivers

           1. Water

              a. Drinking

              b. Cleaning

              c. Irrigation

           2. Irrigation – farming
```

Note Taking

4. Begin with a <u>heading</u>.

- Establish the <u>habit</u> of writing a heading on every page of notes.

  If papers become detached or lost, a student's name in the heading will help recover them.

  If the heading includes information about the content, then notes can be organized easily when writing a paper or studying for a test.

- Think of the <u>5 Ws</u> to remember the parts of a heading: <u>who</u> (name), <u>what</u> (subject), <u>when</u> (date), <u>where</u> (source, page range), and <u>why</u> (topic).

- On the first page of a note-taking assignment, include the <u>name</u>, <u>subject</u> (English, Science, Social Studies), <u>date</u>, <u>source</u> (title of textbook, handout, website), <u>page range</u>, and <u>topic</u>.

- Be consistent with the format: for example, write the name and date on the upper-left; subject, source, and page range on the upper-right; and topic in the center.

- On subsequent pages, <u>rewrite</u> only the name and topic.

- <u>Number</u> the pages of notes for each assignment. *See Sample F.*

5. Determine pertinent <u>main ideas</u>.

- Recognizing a main idea – a <u>broad concept</u> or <u>central theme</u> – provides a frame of reference for assembling related information. Details – smaller facts and ideas – support a main idea. This process of categorizing information helps the student understand, learn, and remember.

- Before taking notes, <u>preview</u> the subject matter to gain a general idea of the content and a sense of its organization.

  Skim selections from textbooks, encyclopedias, and websites to assess the breakdown of information – levels of main ideas: <u>titles</u>, <u>subtitles</u>, <u>chapter</u> names, <u>topics</u>, <u>subtopics</u>, and <u>topic sentences</u> (often the first sentence of a paragraph).

  To preview novels and other types of literature, read <u>dust jackets</u>, <u>prefaces</u>, and <u>introductions</u>.

- Divide reading material into <u>manageable parts</u>. Try to read a whole part first, then go back to take notes. The amount of text a student can handle is variable and a matter of choice:

F: Format

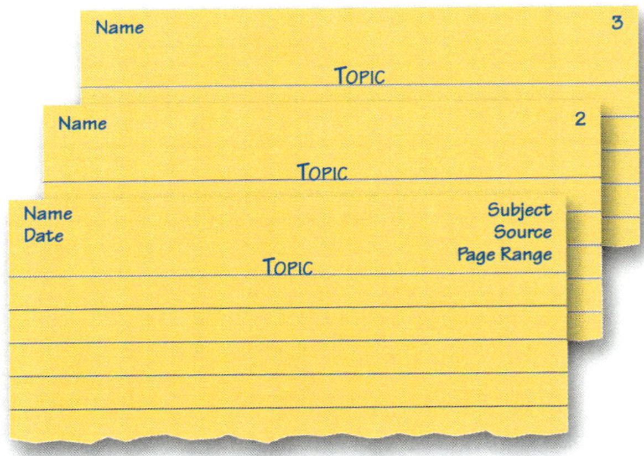

Samples: Main Ideas and Details

G: Science Paragraph

Text

<u>WATER</u> All living things require water to carry out their life processes. Water also makes up a large part of the bodies of most organisms. Your body, for example, is about 65 percent water. A watermelon consists of more than 95 percent water! Water is particularly important to plants and algae. These organisms use water, along with sunlight and carbon dioxide, to make food in a process called photosynthesis (foh toh SIN thuh sis). Other living things eat the plants and algae to obtain energy.

<u>SUNLIGHT</u> Because sunlight is necessary for photosynthesis, it is an important…

–Fred Holtzclaw, Linda Cronin Jones, Ph.D., and Steve Miller, *Science Explorer: Environmental Science*

Notes

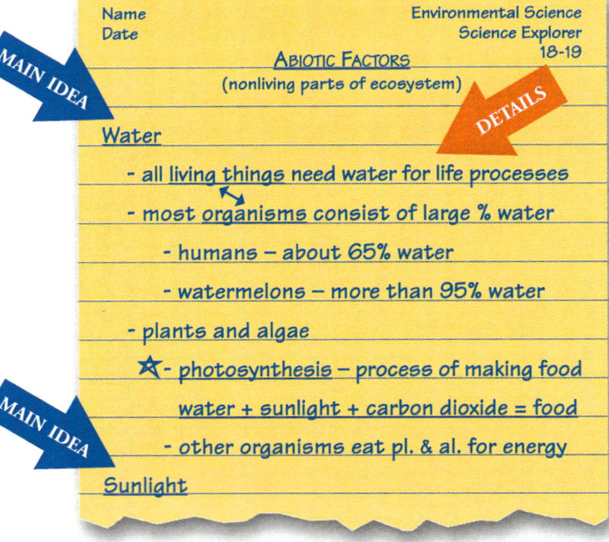

Note Taking

Reading an <u>entire chapter</u> before taking notes is an option.

Working with <u>one paragraph</u> at a time may be preferred.

- When ready to take notes, identify the first <u>important main idea</u>. Sometimes it requires making an inference (drawing a conclusion) because it is implied, not directly stated. For an informal outline, write the main idea on the <u>left</u> and <u>underline</u> it.

- Next the details are written under the main idea. *See Samples G & H.*

6. Identify important <u>details</u>.

- A detail (a smaller <u>fact</u> or <u>idea</u>) can be found in <u>text</u> or <u>illustrations</u> – charts, maps, pictures.

- Find the details that support a main idea.

- Under a main idea, <u>indent</u> and set off the details with <u>dashes</u>, which signal the beginning of the entry, especially when the text is on more than one line.

- Try to use <u>single words or phrases</u>. (Some students may have to write in full sentences until they learn how to write in phrase form.)

- Give each detail its own line or lines.

- <u>Break down information</u> further by indenting again and inserting dashes.

- When defining a <u>new term</u>, write it <u>first</u>. Then follow with the definition or description. Students can underline, highlight, or box in a term, so it stands out.

- <u>Abbreviate</u> familiar words, and <u>use symbols</u> when possible to save time and space. (The texting generation is familiar with this practice.) Be consistent, and make sure the notes can be understood later.

- Be <u>accurate</u>, so the correct spelling will carry over into other writing assignments and tests.

- When taking notes for a writing assignment that requires documentation of sources, write down <u>identifying information</u> (author, page) next to the corresponding entries to relocate sources if needed and when creating a bibliography. *See Samples G & H.*

H: Social Studies Chapter

CLASS NOTES

7. Be <u>prepared</u> to take notes in class.

- Sitting through a class feeling lost is demoralizing. Complete the assigned reading and written homework, and review classroom notes from the day before to have the <u>background</u> for new information.

- If questions about the subject matter come to mind while doing homework or reviewing class notes, jot them down, and try to ask the teacher before new material is introduced.

- Have <u>supplies</u> ready (pens, notebook, laptop).

8. Practice <u>listening</u> techniques.

- It requires a <u>conscious effort</u> to take effective notes, which differs from the passive attention used for watching television, for example.

- Listen for <u>trigger words and phrases</u> that signal important information will follow: "This will be on the test…," "The results were…," "Two reasons for…."

- Watch the teacher. <u>Body language</u> can indicate the importance of information: writing a list on the board, pointing to written information, using hands for emphasis, extended eye contact with the class.

- Recognize when the mind wanders. <u>Refocus</u> on the teacher.

- Distinguish between different types of material and their <u>levels of importance</u>:

  For example, when material is <u>introduced</u>, pay close attention and listen carefully.

  When a lesson is <u>reviewed</u> (and the student feels confident about the material), listening does not have to be as intense.

- The student's <u>position in the classroom</u> can help reduce distractions and create an environment that is conducive to learning. Try to sit in close proximity to the teacher and the boards (black, white, and smart). If possible, avoid sitting near disruptive students.

- <u>Posture</u> should be relaxed but upright. Slouching breeds inattention and may be interpreted by the teacher as disinterest.

9. <u>Take notes</u> in class.

- Although the <u>format</u> for taking notes in class is the same as it is for taking notes from reading material, the circumstances are different.

- Taking notes in class involves performing several behaviors at the same time: listening, sifting through information, participating, and writing.

- Start with a <u>heading</u> that includes name, date, subject, and topic.

  Be consistent with the <u>format</u>: for example, <u>name</u> and <u>date</u> on the <u>upper-left</u>; <u>subject</u> on the <u>upper-right</u>; and <u>topic</u> in the <u>center</u>. Write <u>Class Notes</u> under the subject on the <u>upper-right</u> to distinguish them from other note-taking sources.

  It is easier to remember the parts of a heading if they are written in the same place. Also, a consistent format is helpful when organizing notes to write a paper or study for a test,

- <u>Number</u> subsequent pages and label with name and topic.

- Try to leave <u>space</u> around notes by <u>skipping lines</u> or creating <u>wide margins</u>, so information can be added later if necessary.

- The <u>process</u> for taking notes in class is as follows:

  While keeping the topic in mind, listen for the <u>key main ideas</u>.

  Write a main idea next to the <u>left margin</u> and <u>underline</u> it, so it stands out.

  Follow a main idea with the <u>relevant details</u> that support it.

  <u>Indent</u> and set off the details with <u>dashes</u>.

  Give each detail its own line or lines.

  Break down information further by indenting again and inserting dashes.

  Write specific <u>terms first</u> and follow with their definitions.

  Use <u>single words or phrases</u> as often as possible.

  <u>Abbreviate</u> familiar words.

- During class, a teacher may skip around or add onto previously given information. Students must adapt.

  <u>Leave space</u> around notes for added information. If necessary, draw an arrow to the insertion point.

  Even though a piece of information has been written as a detail in the notes, it can be pulled out and repeated as a main idea (in the left margin, underlined), giving the student more space to expand on a point that the teacher decides to develop.

- Copy information from the <u>board</u>, including pictures, charts, tables.

- Remember that good information can come from <u>students</u>. Be sure the teacher confirms its accuracy.

- Do not hesitate to ask the teacher to <u>repeat</u> or <u>explain</u> information.

- <u>Customize</u> notes to emphasize points:

  Make <u>symbols</u> – stars, arrows, equal signs.

  Draw <u>frames</u> – circles, boxes, clouds.

  <u>Underline</u> or highlight.

  Use different <u>colored pens</u> or markers.

  Make a <u>picture</u> when helpful.

Picture Notes

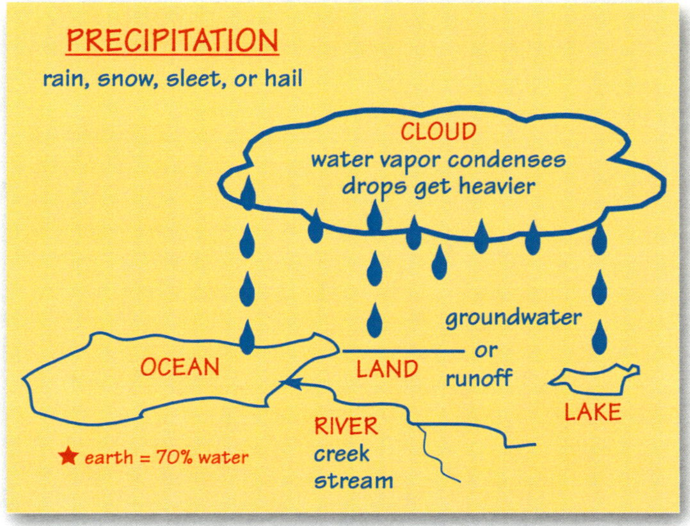

I: Science Class Lecture

Spoken Text

*As more and more **water vapor** condenses, the drops of water in a **cloud** become larger and heavier. Eventually, these drops fall back to Earth in the form of **rain**, **snow**, **sleet**, or **hail**. This **PRECIPITATION** falls mostly on bodies of water. Why? Because **water covers about 70% of our planet**. The rest falls on land, either soaking into the soil by the force of gravity and becoming **groundwater** or running downhill, which is called **runoff** – towards creeks, streams, rivers, and finally back to oceans.*

Note Taking

- Taking notes in class often requires <u>quick thinking and writing</u>. Remember that adjustments can be made later.

- The goal is to understand class notes when reviewing them. As soon as possible, <u>look over</u> the notes to <u>correct</u>, <u>clarify</u>, or <u>rewrite</u> information.

- Rewriting notes is a valuable strategy for <u>reinforcing content</u> and <u>preparing for tests</u>.
  See Samples I & J.

J: Psychology Class Notes – Rewritten

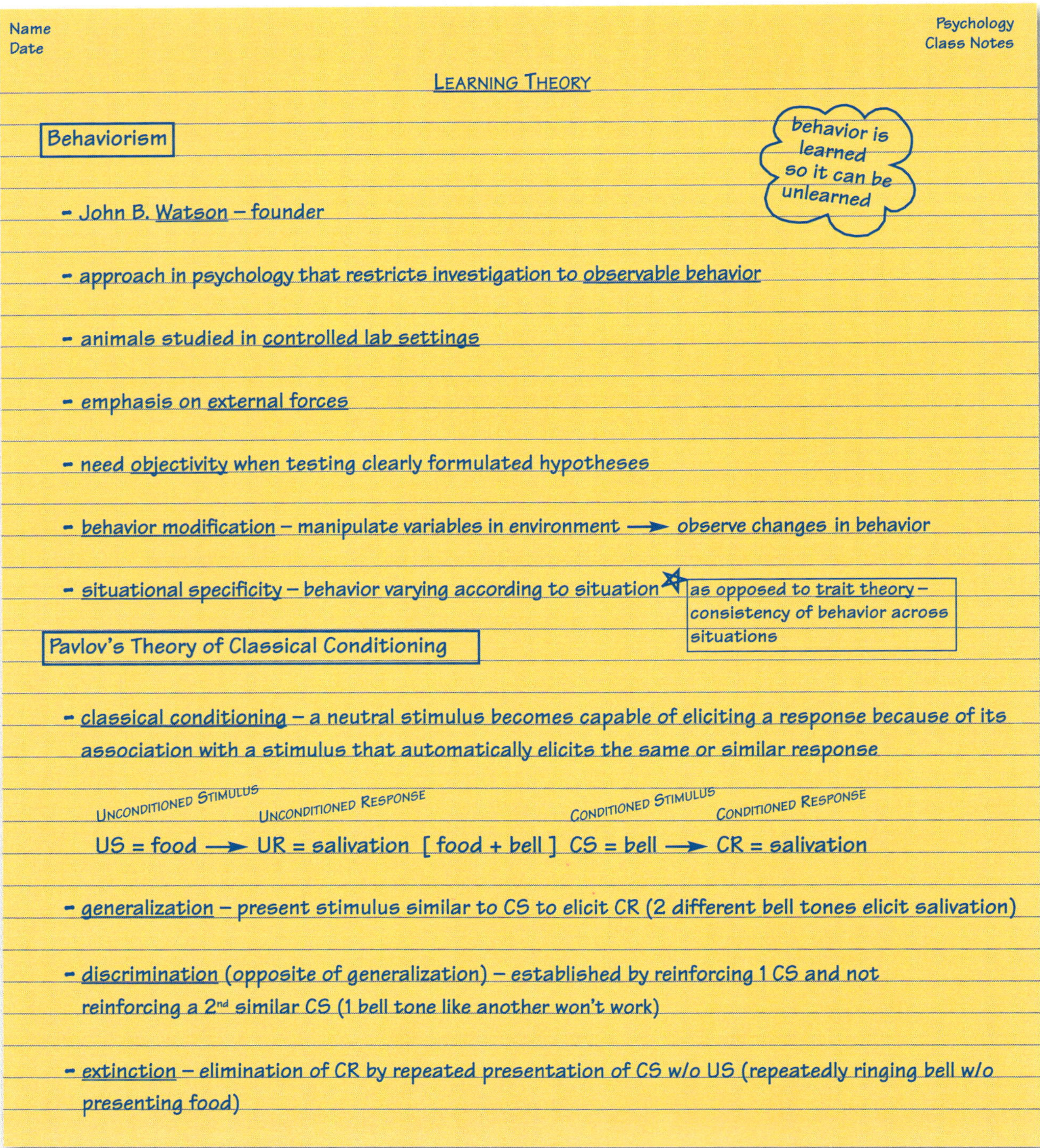

ANNOTATION

10. Take notes within the text of reading material.

- Annotating – writing comments or explanations on a page – brings to the fore important aspects of the reading.

- It includes writing notes in the margins as well as highlighting, underlining, and circling parts of the existing text.

- Consider the following suggestions when annotating text:

  Underline main ideas.

  Define unknown terms.

  Draw attention to characters and their roles in a narrative.

  Mark important themes and interesting passages.

  Jot down ideas or interpretations.

  Point out symbolism (metaphors, similes, imagery).

  Write short summaries at the end of chapters or where needed.

- Incorporate the teacher's comments in the notes.

- Compare notes with the teacher's comments to check for accuracy.
  See Sample K.

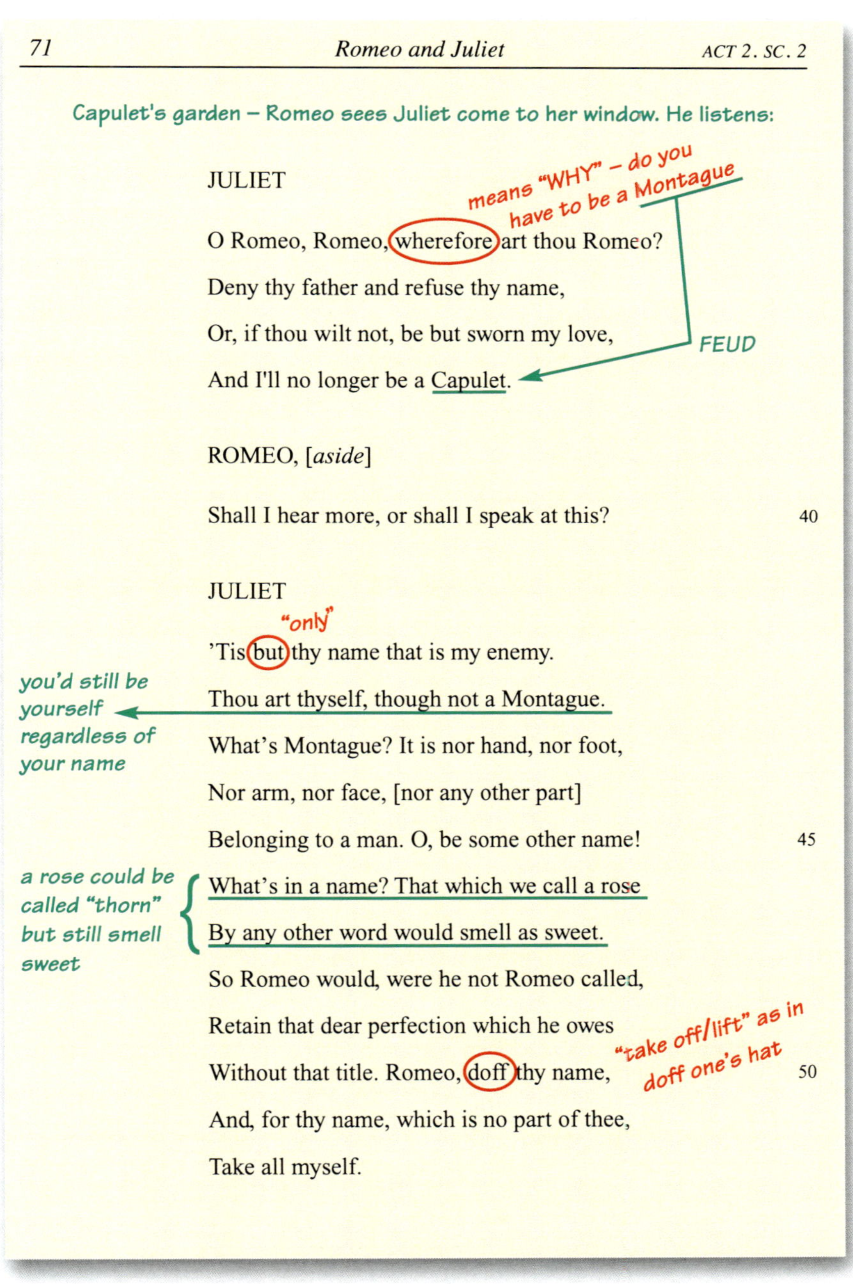

Sample: Annotated Text

K: English – Play

– William Shakespeare, *Romeo and Juliet,* edited by Barbara A. Mowat and Paul Werstine

Preparing for tests involves both short- and long-term strategies. If solid study habits are established from the beginning, then getting ready for a test will be more manageable and even gratifying. Try the techniques described in this section to improve the process of studying.

LONG-TERM STRATEGIES

1. Organize schoolwork.

- Establishing a manageable system for organizing different kinds of schoolwork makes test preparation easier.

- There are various supplies that can help keep schoolwork organized: loose-leaf (three-ring) binders, spiral notebooks, folders.

- A practical choice is the loose-leaf binder because material can be added and removed as needed.

- The amount and type of material from each class should determine the size of binders and whether to use one for each subject or one for several subjects.

- Divide a school subject into sections that contain different kinds of schoolwork: Homework, Notes/Handouts, Tests/Quizzes, Papers/Projects.

- Another method is to integrate all types of schoolwork within a subject by date (eliminating the need for sections).

- Spiral notebooks are also an option. They are light to carry and easy to use. They come with dividers, pockets, and other features that can accommodate all kinds of schoolwork.

- Establish a filing system in a cabinet, drawer, or box that will color coordinate with notebooks. Use color-coordinated hanging files and file folders.
  See Samples A, B, & C.

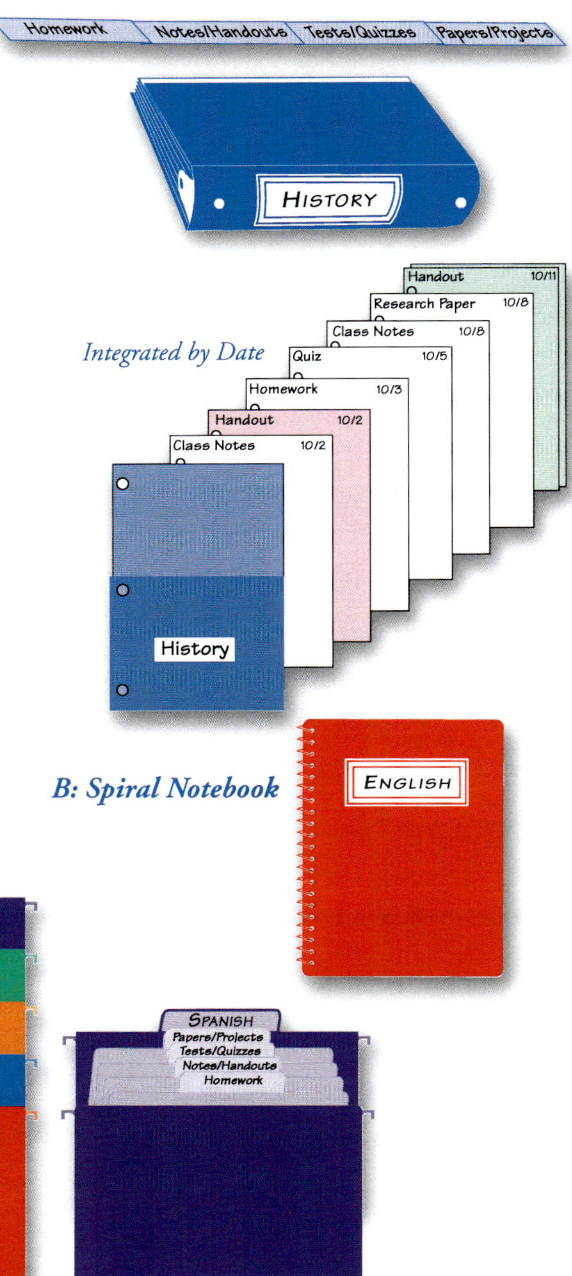

2. Set up an organized study environment.

- A study environment should not impede a student's ability to focus. For one student, a desk in a quiet room is ideal. For another, especially a younger student, this setting may be too isolating.

- Advise the student to choose a space that is comfortable and conducive to learning. The choice should be determined by the student's needs and the type of homework.

- Help the student identify tasks that require intense concentration (reading and taking notes, preparing an outline, writing a report) and try to eliminate distractions.

- Have school supplies at hand.

- Clean out the backpack periodically, and file papers that may be needed later to study for a final exam.

3. Manage time effectively.

- Expose younger students to the practice of scheduling activities. Make a list together: time to wake up, to do homework, to play with a friend.

- Older students should get into the habit of writing their assignments in a date book. Include significant extracurricular activities. Electronic planners can be helpful, but be aware that schools often limit their use.

- Keep a monthly calendar at home. Record the due dates of long-term assignments, major tests, and special events as an overview of these important dates.

- The monthly calendar is a reminder to plan ahead:

  Anticipate a special event by planning to do homework in advance.

  Break down long-term assignments into smaller tasks.

  Schedule sufficient study times for major tests.

  Write times in the weekly date book to work ahead.

  See Samples D & E.

D: Weekly Date Book

E: Monthly Calendar

4. Practice good work habits.

- The student's very first assignment is to recognize and adapt to the teacher's individual style and expectations. When the teacher hands out a syllabus or discusses requirements for the class – homework, note taking, tests – be alert.

- Keep up with homework.

- Take notes in class and on reading assignments. When appropriate, highlight or annotate the text of a book, handout, article.

- Rewrite class notes in a clear format to reinforce the material.

- If there is no time to rewrite class notes, at least look them over before the next class.

- Build an index-card file for vocabulary words, specialized terms, math facts.

  (For more about index cards: Step 10)

- Correct homework, notes, and tests, so the information is accurate.

- Ask questions in class when clarification is needed, and make an appointment to work with the teacher if something is still unclear.

- If absent, get notes from a reliable student, and catch up as soon as possible.

SHORT-TERM STRATEGIES

5. Prepare for a test in advance.

- Guard against becoming overwhelmed by too much material to study at one time.

- Know what material will be covered (chapters in a textbook, handouts, past quizzes).

- Estimate the overall time needed to study. The amount of material and the weight of the grade will determine the timetable.

- Here are some ways to break down the material into manageable parts:

  Tackle the content of one chapter at a time. Coordinate notes, handouts, quizzes, and other tests that cover the same topic.

  Separate a subject into its different areas. For English or a foreign language, work separately on vocabulary, grammar, literature.

  Divide the work by time frames. Begin two weeks before a test, study 45 minutes every other day, and reserve several hours during the weekends.

- Plan times to study, and write a schedule in the date book.

- Consider varying study locations. Studying in different locations can keep the mind alert.

6. Pay attention to the <u>teacher</u>.

- Use <u>review sheets</u> and <u>study guides</u> provided by the teacher.
- Find out the <u>components</u> of a test (multiple choice, short answer, essay).
- Attend <u>review sessions</u>, and listen carefully. Take notes, be an active participant, and ask well-defined questions.
- Make an <u>appointment</u> to see the teacher individually, if needed.

7. Organize <u>notes</u>.

- Remember that notes are taken in the <u>classroom</u> and from <u>reading material</u> – textbooks, handouts, the Internet.
- Teachers may provide their own notes in the form of a <u>study guide</u>.
- Try to coordinate the notes from these different sources, so <u>one topic</u> can be studied at a time.

8. Develop a <u>study guide</u>.

- Preparing a study guide is beneficial for several reasons:

  As information is gathered and written out, understanding is reinforced.

  Once the study guide is complete, it becomes a <u>review tool</u> for the upcoming exam.
- Assemble information from all <u>pertinent sources</u>: class notes, notes from the textbook and handouts, previous tests and quizzes.
- If a <u>course outline</u> is handed out at the beginning of the term, refer to it, and include all relevant material in the study guide.
- Write the topic as the heading at the top of the page. The rest of the layout will follow in <u>two columns</u>.
- List a <u>term</u> (specialized word or expression) in the <u>left column</u>, and underline it.
- Write its <u>definition or explanation</u> in the <u>right column</u>, which should be wider to accommodate more text.
- Sometimes, a term requires several details to define it. <u>Indent</u> and write a word that will <u>prompt</u> the appropriate information – advantages, disadvantages, results.
- When studying, cover the right column, and expose the answers one by one. This format makes it easy for students to test themselves.
  See Sample F.

Sample: Study Guide

F: Terms and Definitions

Science 8
Study Guide

TERMS   <u>ENERGY RESOURCES</u>   **DEFINITIONS**

Term	Definition
<u>fuel</u>	matter that can provide energy through chemical reaction
<u>energy</u>	heat, light, electricity, motion
<u>Einstein</u>	$E=mc^2$
<u>fossil fuels</u>	coal, oil, natural gas
<u>source</u>	made from dead organisms from hundreds of millions of years ago
<u>reserves</u>	fossil fuel deposits
<u>nonrenewable</u>	resource that can be used up (fossil fuels vs sun, wind, water)
<u>hydrocarbons</u>	energy-rich chemical compounds containing carbon & hydrogen
	fossil fuels have more hydrocarbons per kg than most other fuels
<u>combustion</u>	process of burning fuel
<u>formula</u>	carbon & hydrogen atoms + oxygen (from air) = carbon dioxide & water → energy (heat & light)
<u>energy conversion</u>	burning of gasoline → chemical → thermal → mechanical
<u>coal</u>	solid black mineral formed from remains of plants
<u>major use</u>	to fuel electric power plants
<u>mining</u>	process of removing minerals from ground
<u>advantages</u>	abundant in US
	relatively easy to transport
	provides lots of energy
	have improved equipment and safety
<u>disadvantages</u>	accidents in mines
	black lung disease (coal dust)
	increased erosion
	water pollution from runoff
	air pollution from burning
<u>oil/petroleum</u>	thick, black liquid from remains of small ocean animals, algae & protists
<u>source</u>	found underground in sandstone/limestone
<u>drilling</u>	use sound waves to locate oil; oil rigs pump from ground
<u>advantages</u>	petro chemicals – medicines, plastics, cosmetics, paints

9. Plan for <u>possible essay</u> questions.

- Look over the study guide, and try to recall what the teacher emphasized or expanded on in class. Consider main ideas that could incorporate a significant amount of relevant information. These subjects are likely choices for essay questions.

- Write some <u>sample</u> essay questions.

- For each question, develop a <u>thesis statement</u>, and construct a short, <u>informal outline</u> of pertinent information.

- Even if the essay questions on the test are different, content will likely overlap. Students can adapt and apply much of the information prepared and studied.
  See Sample G.

Sample: Possible Essays

G: Question, Thesis, and Informal Outline

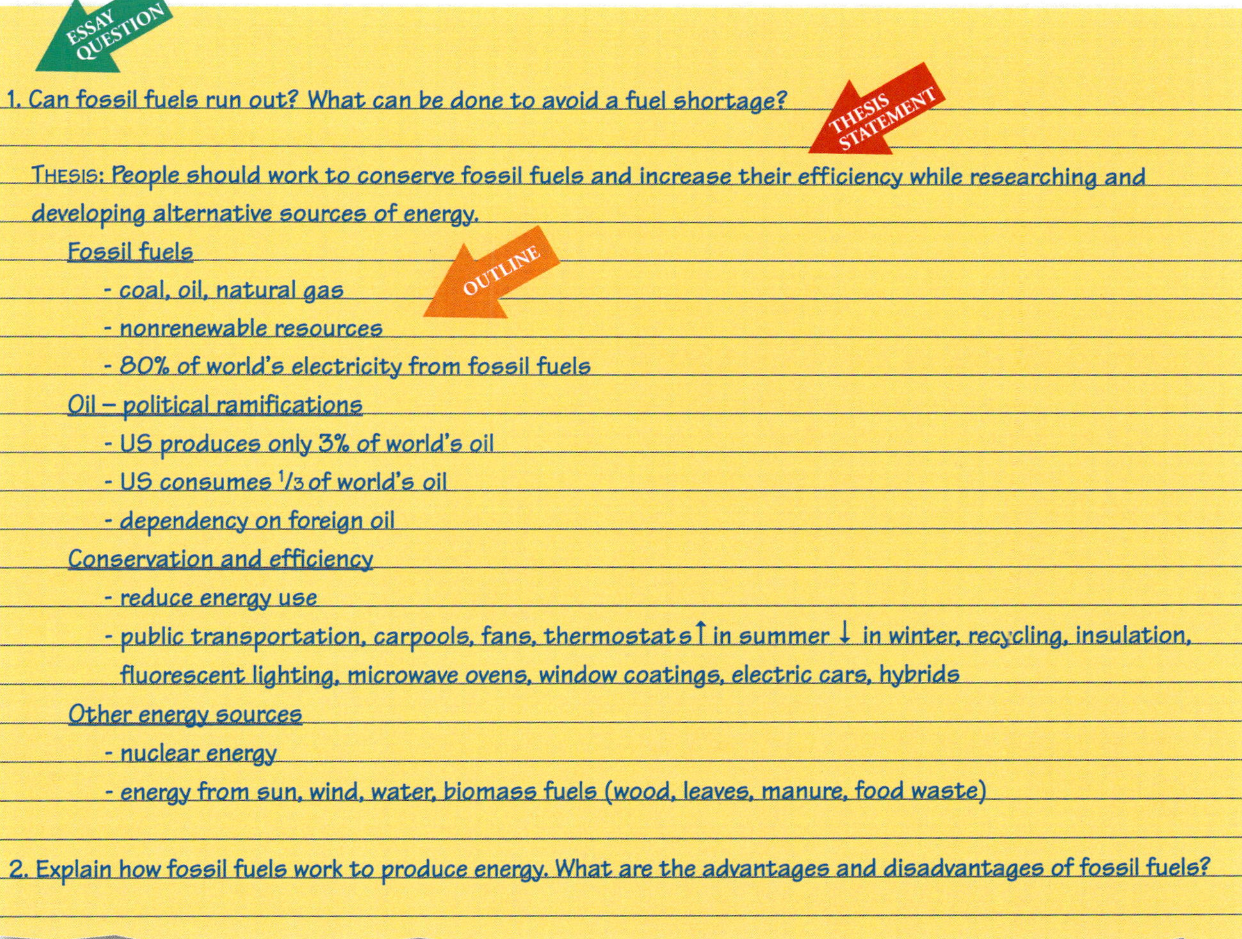

10. Transfer information onto <u>index cards</u>.

- Certain kinds of material contain independent, <u>short pieces of information</u> that can be easily written on index cards. Look at the following examples:

  Write a <u>vocabulary word</u> on one side of an index card and its <u>definition</u> on the other side.

  Write <u>foreign language verbs</u> on one side and their respective <u>conjugations</u> on the other.

  Write <u>math facts</u> and <u>science formulas</u> in the same way.

- More <u>extensive material</u> can be condensed and divided into smaller parts for index cards:

  Short <u>summaries</u> of literary pieces.

  Bullet-point <u>lists</u> of the causes of historic events.

  Concise <u>explanations</u> of scientific experiments.

- Shuffle the index cards, and use them as <u>flash cards</u> to recall and memorize information. Make duplicates, and play a game of concentration.

- <u>Collect and file</u> the index cards throughout the year to use when studying for tests and final exams.

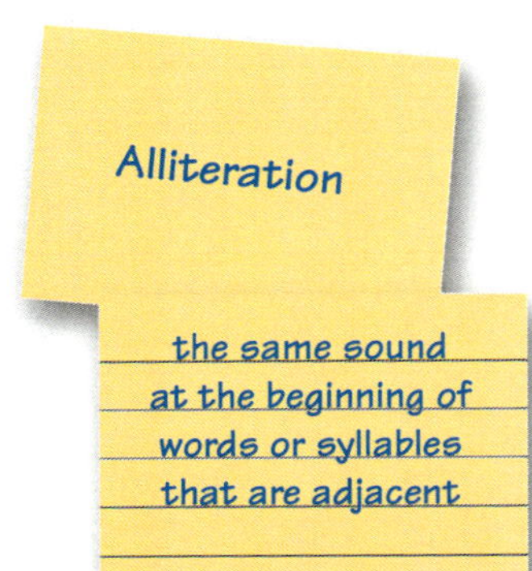

11. Use the <u>computer</u>.

- The <u>Internet</u> is an excellent resource for test preparation. Visit websites that teachers recommend and other students find helpful.

- Type the subject and grade level into a <u>search engine</u>, and find websites with study guides, worksheets, practice quizzes.

- Become familiar with credible <u>websites</u> (math.com, encarta.msn.com, collegeboard.com) and <u>live help</u> online through libraries and other educational institutions.

- <u>Software</u> is available to help students learn and practice skills (*Kid Pix, Typing Tutor, Where in the World is Carmen Sandiego?*).

12. Remember through <u>meaning</u>.

- The more a student understands information, the easier it is to remember.

- Whether trying to learn <u>rote material</u>, such as math facts, or <u>complex information</u>, such as the process of photosynthesis, <u>understanding the concepts</u> is key.

- Tackle difficult material by <u>rereading</u>. Break down information into <u>smaller parts</u>, and focus on one at a time. Think through the parts while saying the information out loud, draw a picture, or use <u>visualization</u> techniques:

  "Why do we have day and night?"

  When the side of the Earth where we live is facing the Sun, it is day, and when the Earth is turned away from the Sun, it is night.

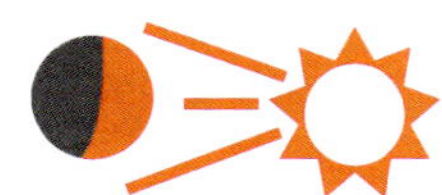

- Connect subject matter to <u>examples</u> whenever possible to reveal or clarify meaning and to develop the ability to apply knowledge.

- In and outside the classroom, students should be <u>active learners</u>, developing listening skills, participating in discussions, and pursuing interests.
  See Sample H.

Sample: Memory through Meaning

H: Using Examples

INFORMATION: *The center of gravity* is the point where the mass of an object can be equally balanced.

EXAMPLE: **Do this:** Balance a pencil on a finger.

APPLICATION: Now the student can learn about levers.

INFORMATION: *Alliteration* is the repetition of the first sound in two or more adjacent words or syllables.

EXAMPLE: **Say this:** <u>P</u>eter <u>P</u>iper <u>p</u>icked a <u>p</u>eck of <u>p</u>ickled <u>p</u>eppers…

APPLICATION: Now the student can identify this stylistic device in literature.

INFORMATION: *Multiplication* is adding the same number a certain number of times.

EXAMPLE: **Look at this:**

$$3 \times 4 = 12 \quad |||\ +\ |||\ +\ |||\ +\ |||\ =\ ||||||||||||$$
$$3\ +\ 3\ +\ 3\ +\ 3\ =\ 12$$

$$4 \times 3 = 12 \quad ||||\ +\ ||||\ +\ ||||\ =\ ||||||||||||$$
$$4\ +\ 4\ +\ 4\ =\ 12$$

APPLICATION: Now the student can compute other multiplication facts and solve word problems that require multiplication. Even memorizing the times tables will be easier.

13. Remember with mnemonic devices.

- Mnemonic devices are <u>association techniques</u> that can trigger memory:

  Remember how to spell the endings of the homonyms principal/principle.
  Think: "The princi<u>pal</u> is my pal."

  A famous character in science helps students remember the order of colors in the spectrum.
  Think: "<u>R</u>oy <u>G</u>. <u>B</u>iv" for <u>R</u>ed, <u>O</u>range, <u>Y</u>ellow, <u>G</u>reen, <u>B</u>lue, <u>I</u>ndigo, <u>V</u>iolet.

  Many music students remember the notes on a treble staff this way.
  Think: "<u>E</u>very <u>G</u>ood <u>B</u>oy <u>D</u>oes <u>F</u>ine" for the lines and "<u>F A C E</u>" for the spaces.

  To remember the order of operations in mathematical expressions, use an acronym.
  Think: "P E M D A S" for <u>P</u>arentheses, <u>E</u>xponents, <u>M</u>ultiplication/<u>D</u>ivision, <u>A</u>ddition/<u>S</u>ubtraction.

  A common rhyme helps students remember when Columbus sailed to the New World.
  Think: "In 1492, Columbus sailed the ocean blue."

- Students can <u>make up</u> their own mnemonic devices, which is effective because they are personal and reflect the way a student's mind works.

- When dealing with a large number of items, it is helpful to divide them into <u>smaller groups</u>:

  For example, in order to memorize the 12 countries of South America, divide them into two parts and create a mnemonic device for each. Two groups of six countries will be easier to remember.

  Work with a cluster of countries, such as <u>B</u>razil, <u>B</u>olivia, <u>P</u>araguay, <u>C</u>hile, <u>A</u>rgentina, and <u>U</u>ruguay.

  The student moves around the first letters of the countries until they make up the acronyms PAC BUB. Next, the student thinks:
  "The time has come for my first trip to South America, so I better pac [pack] Bub, my favorite stuffed animal."

14. Study and test memory.

- The process of studying involves checking memory.

- Regardless of how the material is broken down, <u>review</u> the information already studied before moving on. For example, study Chapter 1, then test memory before moving on to Chapter 2. After studying Chapter 2, test memory of Chapters 1 and 2 before studying Chapter 3, and so on. Study and test until the information is remembered correctly. This process helps to reinforce memory and decrease test anxiety.

- Here are some ways to test memory:

  <u>Think</u> through the material, either silently or out loud. Then look back, and check for accuracy. Study more if necessary.

  <u>Make up questions</u>, and write down the answers. Check for accuracy.

  Have <u>someone else ask</u> questions. Again, repeat until all the answers are correct.

  <u>Teach</u> someone else the material. Check for accuracy.

15. Approach a test with specific strategies in mind.

- The <u>night before</u> a test, gather together school <u>supplies</u> needed (pencils, pens, calculator).
- Get a good night's <u>sleep</u>, and on the day of the test, <u>eat</u> a <u>healthy</u> breakfast and lunch.
- Students sometimes forget to write their <u>names</u> on a test. Do this right away.
- Always <u>read directions</u> carefully.

- Look over the <u>entire test</u>, and size up what is expected.

- After scanning the <u>types of questions</u> and their <u>point values</u>, decide how to proceed. For example, if the true-or-false questions are worth one point each, while the short-answer questions are five points each, work on the five-point section first.

- Here are some strategies for <u>multiple-choice</u> questions:

  Read all the possibilities.

  Eliminate wrong answers.

  Make the best choice. Remember, there can be more than one right answer from which to choose. For example, think about this question – How many stars are in the sky? [hundreds? thousands? millions?] Choose the best answer. [millions]

- Here are some strategies for <u>true-or-false</u> questions:

  Identify absolute words (always, every, only). These words require the statement to be true 100% of the time; therefore, the answer is <u>less likely to be true</u>.

  Pay attention to indefinite words (sometimes, frequently, generally, etc.). These words do not require the statement to be true 100% of the time; the answer, therefore, is <u>more likely to be true</u>.

  Look for negatives (no, not, cannot, etc.). Drop the negative, decide whether the statement is true or false, then reverse it for the correct answer.

- For an <u>essay</u>, analyze the question and plan ahead:

  Does the question have <u>parts</u>? They can help organize an essay.

  Are there <u>directives</u> (compare, describe, evaluate)? They will determine the focus of an essay.

  Is an <u>opinion</u> required? A thesis statement should incorporate the student's point of view.

  Underline <u>key information</u> in the question. Refer back to the question to answer it fully.

  Develop a <u>thesis statement</u> that defines the purpose of the essay.

  Jot down <u>main ideas</u> and supporting <u>details</u> pertinent to the thesis in the margins or on scrap paper.

  <u>Number</u> the main ideas so they correspond to the question and unfold in a logical sequence.

  Begin writing the essay with an <u>introduction</u>. Include the thesis statement as the last sentence.

  Follow with the essay's <u>body paragraphs</u>. Refer to the list of main ideas and details.

  Look at the question again and read through the <u>entire essay</u>. With the facts and focus in mind, formulate a conclusion.

  Write a <u>conclusion</u>. Remember to summarize what the essay has proven, and express an interesting idea that derives from the content. Make a decisive impression.

- If the test has been completed with <u>time to spare</u>, resist the urge to leave:

  <u>Review</u> the test to make sure all questions are answered, none are mismarked, and mistakes are corrected.

  <u>Proofread</u> for spelling, punctuation, decimal points, etc.

- Standardized tests like the SATs and ACTs require particular strategies. Check the library, Internet, and prep courses.
  See Sample I.

Test Preparation

I: Planning for an Essay

Describe how a <u>nuclear power plant</u> produces <u>electrical energy</u>. Do you think we should <u>build more</u> <u>nuclear power plants</u>? Explain <u>why or why not</u>.

② - nuclear power plants
- controlled fission reaction ⟶ heat ⟶ boils water ⟶ steam ⟶ turbine ⟶ electricity
- uranium (U-235) fuel
  - neutron shot at nucleus
  - split nucleus releases energy/heat
- containment building
  - reactor vessel – rods (fuel & control), cooling water
  - heat exchanger ⟶ steam
  - turbine ⟶ generator ⟶ electric current
    condenser ⟶ cooling tower
- 20% of US electricity, 70%+ of France

③ - problems
- Chernobyl – meltdown/contamination
- radioactive waste
- safety issues
- costly

① - nuclear reaction
- Einstein (1905) – matter ⟶ energy ($E=mc^2$)
- fission – splitting of atom's nucleus
- uncontrolled – atom bomb/controlled – nuclear power plant

④ - alternatives
- nuclear fusion – cleaner, safer, cheaper
- renewable – sun, wind, water

Unresolved safety issues should deter the proliferation of more nuclear power plants despite the effectiveness of nuclear power as a source of energy.

> **I have a lot of interesting ideas, but I have trouble organizing them."**

One of the most challenging aspects of producing a paper is knowing where to begin and how to proceed. This section breaks down the process of writing an essay into manageable steps, increasing efficiency and improving the quality of work.

1. Choose a <u>topic</u>.

- When a topic is not assigned, choose one that is of <u>personal interest</u>.
- Determine a <u>focus</u>. For example, an essay on Shakespeare's *Macbeth* could focus on the main character's tragic flaw.
- From the focus comes the all-important <u>thesis</u>.
  See Sample A.

2. Write a <u>thesis statement</u>.

- A thesis statement is a concise yet well-developed <u>sentence</u> that identifies the <u>purpose</u> of an essay. It reveals a <u>point of view</u> on a <u>specific idea</u> that is going to be explored.
- Write the thesis statement as the <u>last sentence</u> of the <u>introduction</u>.
- <u>Revise</u> the thesis statement at any time during the process of writing an essay.
- The thesis statement is supported throughout the paper.
  See Sample B.

3. <u>Brainstorm</u> for content.

- Brainstorming enables a student to <u>think</u> without concern for organization, language, or mechanics.
- With the thesis statement in mind, brainstorm <u>facts</u>, <u>ideas</u>, and <u>impressions</u>.
- Entries may come from <u>educational sources</u> (books, articles, the Internet), <u>personal experiences</u>, or <u>original thoughts</u>.
- Make a <u>list</u> of these facts, ideas, and impressions on paper or on the computer.
- Set off each entry with a <u>dash</u> on paper or a bullet on computer.

Sample: 6th-Grade Personal Essay

A: Topic

```
TOPIC:    spring vacation
FOCUS:    trip to Santa Fe
THESIS:   memorable experience
```

B: Thesis Statement

We were filled with expectations, and I wondered how my trip to Santa Fe would be a memorable experience.

C: Brainstorm

SANTA FE
- spring vacation — trip to Santa Fe
- 4:30 a.m. airport
- We learned about the Southwest in 4th grade.
- Bishop's Lodge — red clay buildings
- rooms at lodge
- Bandelier National Monument
- pueblo ruins   (Cheek, 182) SOURCE
- Trader Jack's flea market
- souvenirs
- buffet breakfast
- gym, hot tub, sauna
- skeet shooting — sign-up
- Native American jewelry
- skeet — safety lesson
- fishing — huge trout
- Tom — expert fisherman
- trout for dinner

For samples by older students: Steps 14–16

Essays

- Try to use <u>single words</u> or <u>short phrases</u>, although certain concepts may be easier to express in sentence form.

- If <u>sources</u> are used and <u>citations</u> required, write the names of <u>authors</u> and <u>page numbers</u> next to the corresponding entries in the brainstorm to make documentation easier when writing a draft and preparing a bibliography.

- Teachers usually specify their preferred style of <u>documentation</u>; otherwise, use formal guidelines, such as those established by the Modern Language Association (MLA).
  See Sample C.

4. Identify <u>main ideas and details</u>.

- Read the entries in the brainstorm list. Decide what main ideas emerge – <u>stated</u> or <u>implied</u> (a drawn conclusion from the stated ideas).

- Make sure the main ideas are <u>broad enough</u> to encompass the remaining entries – the details.

- In another column, write the main ideas using a <u>logical sequence</u> or, on the computer, type a separate list of the main ideas.

- Include the <u>introduction</u> and <u>conclusion</u> in the list of main ideas if some of the details apply. Otherwise, brainstorm for those paragraphs separately.
  (For more about introductions and conclusions: Steps 8 & 10)

- Place a <u>different colored dot</u> or different symbol in front of each main idea. If using a computer, apply a different color to each main idea, or print the list and apply color coding to the hard copy.

- At any point in the process, <u>add or eliminate</u> main ideas or details.

- Sometimes, students know their main ideas and corresponding details, so they can develop an <u>outline</u> without having to brainstorm. Even so, do not hesitate to go back to the brainstorm step for parts of the essay.
  (For more about outlines: Step 6)
  See Sample D.

D: Main Ideas & Details

- Trader Jack's flea market
- souvenirs
- buffet breakfast
- gym, hot tub, sauna
- skeet shooting – sign-up
- Native American jewelry
- skeet – safety lesson
- fishing – huge trout
- Tom – expert fisherman
- trout for dinner
- I want to fish at home too.

MAIN IDEAS

- Introduction
- Bishop's Lodge
- Skeet shooting
- Bandelier Monument
- Shopping
- Fishing
- Conclusion

E: Color Coding

SANTA FE

- spring vacation – trip to Santa Fe
- 4:30 a.m. airport
- We learned about the Southwest in 4th grade.
- Bishop's Lodge – red clay buildings
- rooms at lodge
- Bandelier National Monument
- pueblo ruins   (Cheek, 182)
- Trader Jack's flea market
- souvenirs
- buffet breakfast
- gym, hot tub, sauna
- skeet shooting – sign-up
- Native American jewelry
- skeet – safety lesson
- fishing – huge trout
- Tom – expert fisherman
- trout for dinner
- I want to fish at home too.
- skeet shooting – scores
- skeet again – confidence
- cliffs and Native American caves
- inside caves
- Dad asleep – picture
- stream – I slipped
- plane ride home
- We voted on our favorite activity.
- Mom and Molly – Bandelier National Monument
- ladders – 140 ft.   (Cheek, 182)
- Dad and me – fishing

MAIN IDEAS

- Introduction
- Bishop's Lodge
- Skeet shooting
- Bandelier Monument
- Shopping
- Fishing
- Conclusion

SOURCE

5. <u>Code</u> the brainstorm list.

- Evaluate the details, and place a <u>colored dot</u> (or symbol) in front of each entry that corresponds to the appropriate main idea. On the computer, color code the details accordingly.

- Now the list is ready to transform into a simple, informal outline.
  See Sample E.

6. Develop an <u>informal outline</u>.

- Use a new piece of paper, and rewrite the heading on top.

- Write and underline the <u>first main idea</u> – Introduction – next to the left margin.

- Transfer the <u>details</u> from the brainstorm – by color (or symbol) – that correspond to this first main idea, determining a reasonable <u>sequence</u> – chronological, thematic, dramatic.

- <u>Indent</u> and set off each detail with a <u>dash</u>.

- Write the <u>thesis statement</u> as the last entry of the <u>introduction</u>.

- Continue until all the main ideas are listed with their corresponding details ordered beneath them.

- If <u>sources</u> are used, transfer the names of authors and page numbers from the brainstorm.

- On the <u>computer</u>, <u>cut and paste</u> until the details appear under their corresponding main ideas, following the color coding. <u>Indent</u> each detail and insert a <u>bullet</u>. Use automatic outline formatting.
  See Sample F.

7. <u>Add or subtract</u> entries as needed.

- Examine the <u>sequence</u> of main ideas and details. Make changes, if necessary, to ensure continuity.

- Take a look at the <u>number</u> and <u>quality</u> of details for each main idea.

- If a particular main idea is lacking in substance or there are gaps in the <u>flow of information</u>, either eliminate the category altogether, or add more details.

- Refine and <u>modify</u> the outline at any stage.

- <u>Print</u> the outline, so it can be referred to easily when writing the paper.

- If possible, use the computer to input text.

F: Informal Outline

<u>SANTA FE</u>

MAIN IDEA → Introduction: Spring vacation – trip to Santa Fe
DETAILS →
- thinking about our trip
- 4th grade teacher taught about Southwest
- 4:30 a.m. airport
- We were filled with expectations, and I wondered how my trip to Santa Fe would become a memorable experience. ← THESIS STATEMENT

Bishop's Lodge
- red clay buildings
- rooms at lodge
- buffet breakfast
- sauna, hot tub, gym

Skeet shooting
- sign-up
- safety lesson
- gained confidence
- scores

Bandelier National Monument
- pueblo ruins   (Cheek, 182) ← SOURCE
- cliffs and Native American caves
- ladders – 140 ft.   (Cheek, 182)
- inside caves
- Dad asleep – picture
- stream – I slipped

Shopping
- Trader Jack's flea market
- souvenirs for all of us
- Native American jewelry

Fishing
- huge trout
- Tom – expert fisherman
- trout for dinner

Conclusion: Great trip
- plane ride home – voted on favorite activity
- Mom and Molly – Bandelier Nat'l Monument
- Dad and me – fishing
- fishing became a hobby

Essays

8. Write an **introduction**.

- The introductory paragraph includes sentences that identify the <u>topic</u>, <u>focus</u>, and <u>thesis</u> of the essay.

- Refer to the <u>outline</u>. It will supply the content.

- Begin with a <u>sentence</u> about the <u>topic</u>: an attention-grabber that is a fact, quotation, or declaration.

- Include <u>details</u> that provide <u>background</u> information and lead up to the <u>thesis statement</u>, which is written at the end of the introduction.

- Some students may find it easier to write the body paragraphs first and then work on the introduction.
  See Sample G.

9. Follow with **body paragraphs**.

- Body paragraphs make up the <u>core</u> of a paper.

- Begin the first body paragraph with a sentence that states the main idea – a <u>topic sentence</u>.

- Develop the paragraph with the <u>supporting details</u>.

- Make sure the details unfold in a <u>logical sequence</u>, leading to an appropriate <u>ending sentence</u>.

- For the remaining body paragraphs, continue following the outline – from one main idea to the next.

- As the writing proceeds, some new ideas may come up. Include them if they apply.
  See Sample H.

10. End with a **conclusion**.

- A concluding paragraph reviews the paper's main ideas and ends with a personal realization or decisive thought.

- Refer to the <u>outline</u>.

- Begin with an <u>opening sentence</u> that brings the reader back to the <u>focus</u> of the paper.

- <u>Synthesize</u> what the paper has demonstrated, or describe where the information has led the reader.

- Express some <u>special realization</u> or understanding drawn from the content of the paper.

- Make sure that the ending sentence is <u>decisive</u> or <u>thought-provoking</u>.

G: Introduction

H: Body Paragraph

I: Conclusion

- Remember, the conclusion is the final paragraph, so it leaves a <u>lasting impression</u>.

- Once the conclusion is written, the <u>first draft</u> of the paper is complete.
  See Sample I.

11. <u>Revise and edit</u> for the final draft.

- The <u>quality</u> of a paper can improve greatly during the revision process.

- Before making corrections, <u>save</u> the first draft: Santa Fe_DRAFT. Then <u>rename</u> the document Santa Fe_FINAL, and begin the revision process.

- Read the paper silently and <u>out loud</u>.

- If the teacher has provided a <u>rubric</u> to judge the paper, follow it point by point. Familiarity with well-written, well-organized <u>professional texts</u> is essential to evaluate by comparison.

- <u>Scrutinize</u> content, organization, language usage, and mechanics.

- Read for <u>content</u> – the quality, breadth, and depth of information. Even at this stage, sentences can be added to round out the paper.

- Check for <u>organization</u>. Read the topic sentences of each paragraph consecutively to determine whether their sequence is effective.

- Look at <u>language usage</u> and <u>mechanics</u>: transitional words and phrases; descriptive vocabulary; correct grammar, spelling, punctuation, capitalization.

- Use <u>computer tools</u> provided by word-processing programs – <u>grammar and spelling checkers</u>, for example – but do so carefully as some corrections may not be applicable. Also, take advantage of the <u>dictionary</u>, <u>thesaurus</u>, <u>word-count</u>, and <u>footnote</u> features.

- Memorize and use computer <u>keystrokes</u> to cut, copy, paste, and undo. This saves time when editing a paper.
  See Samples J & K.

12. Write a <u>title</u>.

- It is usually best to think of a title after completing the first draft. At this point, the student will have a good sense of the essay as a whole.

- Write a <u>clear</u> and <u>concise</u> title that introduces the <u>subject</u> of the essay and hints at the <u>thesis</u>.

J: Checklist for Revising and Editing

THESIS

- Do I have a clear, well-written thesis statement with a specific point of view?

- Did I support the thesis statement throughout my paper?

CONTENT

- Do I have sufficient information?

- Are each of my main ideas supported by details?

ORGANIZATION

- Do I have an introduction and a conclusion?

- Do my body paragraphs progress in a logical sequence?

LANGUAGE

- Have I used transitional words and phrases, descriptive vocabulary, and a variety of sentence types?

- Have I avoided repetition (unless used intentionally)?

MECHANICS

- Have I used correct grammar, spelling, punctuation, and capitalization?

DOCUMENTATION

- Are my sources documented correctly?

PRESENTATION

- Is the format of my paper correct?

- Have I put a heading on my paper?

- Is my name on it?

- Have I made a cover and/or title page?

K: Keystrokes for Easy Editing

WINDOWS	KEYSTROKES	MAC	KEYSTROKES
CUT	CONTROL – X	CUT	COMMAND – X
COPY	CONTROL – C	COPY	COMMAND – C
PASTE	CONTROL – V	PASTE	COMMAND – V
UNDO	CONTROL – Z	UNDO	COMMAND – Z

- Be <u>creative</u>: The title should be <u>descriptive</u> and attract the reader. At the same time, consider the <u>tone</u> of the essay; a clever, funny title is not always appropriate.

- In the Santa Fe essay, just adding the adjective "memorable" to the title, "My Trip to Santa Fe," adds a little mystery and foreshadows the thesis statement.

- Try to identify the <u>scope</u> of the paper. For example, "The History of Fashion" as a title about the effect of historical events on fashion is too broad and misleading. Consider this alternative: "Fashion as a Mirror of History."
  See Sample L.

13. <u>Customize</u> the presentation.

- If the teacher has not specified the guidelines for presentation, slip the paper into a <u>report cover</u>. This simple step can <u>protect</u> the final product and increase its credibility.

- If appropriate, design a <u>cover</u>, and include <u>graphics</u>, such as charts, illustrations, and photographs.

- Make a <u>positive impression</u>.

14. Look at another <u>introduction</u>.

- This introductory paragraph from an <u>essay</u> about China's history states the topic – Chinese dynasties – and the <u>focus</u> – their cyclical pattern.

- The sentences that follow describe the characteristics of the cycles and lead to the thesis statement.

- The <u>thesis statement</u> narrows down the focus and communicates the <u>purpose</u> of the essay.
  See Sample M.

15. Look at another <u>body paragraph</u>.

- In this body paragraph from a <u>review</u> of a dance performance, the <u>topic sentence</u> introduces the piece under review – Alvin Ailey's "Night Creatures."

- The <u>details</u> describe the performance with vivid language and effective metaphors.
  See Sample N.

L: Titles

Essay on Homer's *The Odyssey*:
"A Journey into Manhood"

Essay on Poe's character as reflected in his writing:
"Edgar Allan Poe: Mad or Just Eccentric?"

Article on dress code in a school newspaper:
"Hair Today, Gone Tomorrow"

Sample: 10th-Grade History Essay

M: Introduction

Throughout the history of China, dynasties have demonstrated their own defining characteristics, but when examined as a whole, a cyclical pattern emerges within each reign. The dynastic cycle reveals a definite rise and fall, with a new power rising at the end of a failing regime. Then follows a peaceful time and a period of growth. Nearing the end of a cycle, conflict generates collapse, and the pattern begins again. During the Mao and Deng dynasties, society underwent policy changes unique to each reign; however, the structure of the dynastic cycle remained.

Sample: 11th-Grade Dance Essay

N: Body Paragraph

The highlight of the program was a piece choreographed to the music of Duke Ellington's "Night Creatures." Every aspect of the performance helped to create the illusion of creatures in the night. The set was dark; in fact, it was black. Then, in the night, metallic unitards shone like lightning bugs; the smooth, glossy fabric also resembled slimy slugs. Creeping and crawling, swooping and scurrying, the dancers' movements echoed the rhythm of the swing beat. **All of these elements came together to capture the essence of "night creatures."**

16. Look at another <u>conclusion</u>.

- In this concluding paragraph from an English <u>essay</u> entitled "Dylan Thomas: The Mystery of Life," the opening sentence brings the reader back to the <u>focus</u> of the essay.

- Then the sentences that follow <u>synthesize</u> the main ideas, communicate a personal <u>realization</u>, and end with a <u>decisive</u> thought.
  See Sample O.

O: Conclusion

Throughout his poetry, Dylan Thomas explores the great mystery of life and death. In his study of the relationship between man, nature, and God, it appears that Thomas was never able to reach enlightenment. Yet, has man ever been able to define God, nature, and man? Are they independent? What is the "universal secret" of creation and destruction (Rosenthal 385)? ***** These questions are as ancient as man himself. Perhaps, Thomas expected too much. **More likely, though, he believed there was no single answer, and maybe it was this revelation that made him even more determined to reach as many conclusions as possible.**

***** *This is a <u>parenthetical reference</u>. The documentation of this source is recorded in the paper's bibliography.*

"Research papers make me nervous, so I procrastinate. I start them too late, and then I really go crazy."

Begin the process right away. Just focus on one task at a time. Follow the step-by-step procedures in this section, and before long, an organized and well-written research paper will be completed.

1. Choose a topic.

- If a topic is not assigned, choose one of interest.

- Library resources, media outlets, or the Internet may be necessary to inspire a topic.

- For a concise overview of possible subjects, browse through a desk encyclopedia, or search for possible topics online. Wikipedia is an ideal web site for this initial task, but do not use it as a credible reference in the research paper.

- Make sure enough sources on a topic are available to satisfy the scope and time frame of the assignment.
  See Sample A.

2. Determine the focus.

- Once a topic is chosen, investigate sources further to determine a focus for the paper.

- Scan dust jackets, tables of contents, introductions, headings, and subheadings to gain ideas for narrowing down the topic.

- Begin thinking about a possible thesis – a specific aspect of the paper's focus.

  (For more about the thesis: Step 5)
  See Sample A.

3. Select sources.

- When searching for information, remember that there are more sources than books and more outlets than the Internet.

- Teachers will probably limit the number of Internet citations that can be used, so students have an opportunity to broaden their research experiences.

- Locate a variety of sources that provide useful and relevant information.
  See Sample B.

A: Topic/Focus/Thesis

Topic:	Hubble Space Telescope
Focus:	history, description, and achievements
Thesis:	Hubble's impact on space exploration and science

B: List of Possible Sources

ALMANACS	MUSIC COMPOSITIONS
BOOKS	NEWSPAPERS
CD ROMS	ON-LINE SOURCES*
CHARTS	PAMPHLETS
DICTIONARIES	PERFORMANCES
ENCYCLOPEDIAS	PERIODICALS
ESSAYS	POEMS
FILMS	RADIO
INTERVIEWS	SHORT STORIES
MAGAZINES	TELEVISION
MAPS	VIDEO RECORDINGS
MICROFILMS	VISUAL ARTS

Not all on-line sources are credible. Make sure the information is amply acknowledged with author's name, title, affiliation, date created, contact information, and evidence of quality control. (Are there peer reviews? Are there references? Is it an official web site of a reputable organization?)

For samples by older students: Steps 13–15

4. Create and code <u>source cards</u>.

- Source cards help to <u>organize and simplify</u> the process of writing a research paper.

- Use one <u>index card</u> for each source. Write the source's <u>identifying information</u> (author, title, publisher) in the <u>documentation style</u> advised by the teacher.

- If the teacher does not supply instructions on the documentation of sources, use <u>formal guidelines</u>, such as those established by the Modern Language Association (MLA), the American Psychological Association (APA), The Chicago Manual of Style.

- Write the <u>library call number</u> (e.g., QB68.E94) in the <u>upper-right</u> corner of a card to be able to locate it again. If a source does not have a call number, write a label that will identify its location (Internet, radio, documentary).

- Put the source cards in <u>alphabetical order</u> by author, or if the author's name is not available, by title.

- <u>Code</u> the source cards consecutively, each one with its own <u>capital letter</u> (A,B,C) in the <u>upper-left</u> corner. These letters represent the sources – <u>source codes</u>.

- Add or eliminate source cards as the research progresses and recode as necessary. These recorded sources become the <u>working bibliography</u>.

- If the student uses an <u>automatic bibliography</u> site on the computer, such as www.EasyBib.com, writing comprehensive source cards is not necessary; just code the source names, and find the rest of the information later when constructing the bibliography.
  See Sample C.

5. Write a <u>thesis statement</u>.

- A thesis statement is a concise, well-developed sentence that identifies the <u>purpose</u> of a paper, revealing a <u>point of view</u> about a <u>specific idea</u>. It is written in the <u>introduction</u>, usually as the last sentence.

- Writing the thesis statement before beginning an outline acts as a <u>filter</u> for information – keeping the content of the paper on course.

- The thesis statement can be revised as research proceeds or during any of the writing stages.
  See Sample D.

*** *Break <u>on-line addresses</u> after a slash.*

D: Thesis Statement

6. Construct and code an <u>outline</u>.

- Look through the sources again. Read information as needed to get a good sense of the main ideas.

- Choose the important main ideas, and list them. They will be the <u>primary divisions</u> of the outline. Use <u>Roman numerals</u> (I., II., III.) to set them apart.

- Include the <u>introduction</u> as the first Roman numeral and the <u>conclusion</u> as the last.

- Break down the primary divisions, using <u>capital letters</u> (A., B., C.) and indent. These are the <u>secondary divisions</u> of the outline.

- When subdividing entries in an outline, every number I must have a II, every letter A must have a B, and so on.

- Use the fewest words necessary for understanding – <u>single words</u> or <u>phrases</u>.

- Write the <u>thesis statement</u> – in sentence form – as the last capital letter of the introduction.

- If material is covered effectively in a particular source, jot down the <u>source code</u> (from the source card) and <u>page number/s</u> in the <u>margin</u> next to the corresponding entry in the outline.

- The combination of a source code and page number/s is the <u>location code</u> (C, 3). Including location codes on the outline can save time when taking notes: "Now I know where I found that great description of black holes."

- A <u>basic outline</u> with primary and secondary divisions may be sufficient, but some projects may require an expanded outline with further subdivisions.

- If an <u>expanded outline</u> is required, carefully read pertinent text to subdivide the basic outline using <u>Arabic numbers</u> (1., 2., 3.) and <u>lower-case letters</u> (a., b., c.). Indent systematically.

- Remember to record location codes (source code and page number/s) in the margins, so important information can be easily tracked.

- <u>Interaction</u> between the <u>sources and outline</u> is essential. As information is coordinated, modify the outline accordingly.

- Using <u>word-processing software</u> that provides automatic outline formats can save time.

See Samples E, F, & G.

E: Main Ideas for Outline

> I. Introduction: Hubble Space Telescope
>
> II. History and description of Hubble
>
> III. Discoveries made by Hubble
>
> IV. Conclusion: Impact of Hubble

F: Basic Outline

> HUBBLE
>
> I. Introduction: Hubble Space Telescope
>   A. Purpose of Hubble   (C, 3)
>   B. Type of telescope
>   C. Thesis statement:
>   The Hubble Space Telescope is a prime example of technological progress in our space program, which has led to new advances in science.
>
> II. History and description of Hubble
>   A. Reason Hubble was built
>   B. Who built it and when
>   C. How it was built
>   D. How it functions
>   E. Major flaw and repair
>
> III. Discoveries made by Hubble
>   A. Neutron stars
>   B. Supernovae
>   C. Comets
>   D. Asteroids
>   E. Evidence of black holes
>
> IV. Conclusion: Impact of Hubble
>   A. Significance of Hubble
>   B. Advances in science

7. Create and code <u>notecards</u>.

- Use the <u>outline</u> to direct the process of taking notes. If important information emerges from the reading that is not in the outline, modify the outline.

- Apply <u>critical reading</u> strategies when taking notes: As source material is read, analyze its relevance, compare it to other authors' ideas, and decide whether it supports the paper's thesis.

- Remember, the information from outside sources is used to help form and support the <u>thesis statement</u>.

- The paper's substance is in the <u>details</u>, so record enough details for sufficient content. When reading, locate details within paragraphs. Details support a <u>main idea</u> found in a <u>topic sentence</u> – often written at the beginning of a paragraph.

- Details are also found in <u>illustrations</u> – charts, graphs, maps, pictures, tables.

- Record the notes on <u>index cards</u>. Write about one piece of information per card, whether it is a fact or an idea.

- Although a notecard covers one point, it can include more than one <u>phrase</u> or <u>sentence</u>. In fact, one idea could require writing a lot of information (a list, for example).

- Use different words than the author's (paraphrase). <u>Paraphrasing</u> at this stage saves time later. When <u>quoting</u> an author's exact words, use quotation marks, and make sure to copy the quotation exactly.

- Whether quoting or paraphrasing, always <u>reference and document</u> the source. <u>Plagiarism</u>, derived from the Latin word for kidnapper, is submitting an author's words or ideas as one's own, whether by intention or accident.

- When personal, <u>analytical thoughts</u> come to mind, write them on notecards.

- Place <u>two codes</u> on each notecard: an outline code and a location code.

- The <u>outline code</u> refers to a section of the outline headed by a <u>Roman numeral</u>. Label the <u>upper-left</u> of each notecard with the Roman numeral that corresponds to the appropriate <u>section</u> of the outline.

G: Expanded Outline – Introduction

** An <u>electronic source</u> may not have numbered pages. Just write down the source code (A).*

H: Notecards

- Remember, the <u>location code</u> refers to a source code and page number/s (C, 3). Place the location code in the <u>lower-right</u> corner of each card. (Some or all of these codes have been written in the margin of the outline.)

- Continue to take notes until enough information is collected. The number of cards depends upon the scope of the paper.
See Sample H.

8. <u>Sequence</u> the notecards.

- <u>Group</u> the notecards according to their <u>outline codes</u> (I's together, II's together, III's together).

- Within each group, <u>order</u> the cards by referring to the subdivisions in the outline and using personal judgment.

- If there are gaps in content, continue researching the topic, and write <u>additional information</u> onto new cards. Set aside cards that seem irrelevant.

- When the notecards are sequenced in each group, stack the groups in order, and number the cards from beginning to end in the <u>upper-right corner</u>. This <u>sequence code</u> ensures that order can be restored easily.
See Sample I.

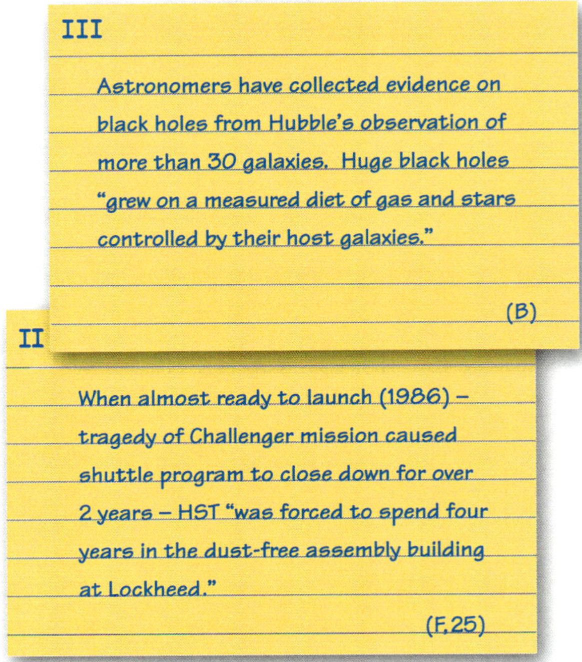

I: Sequenced Notecards

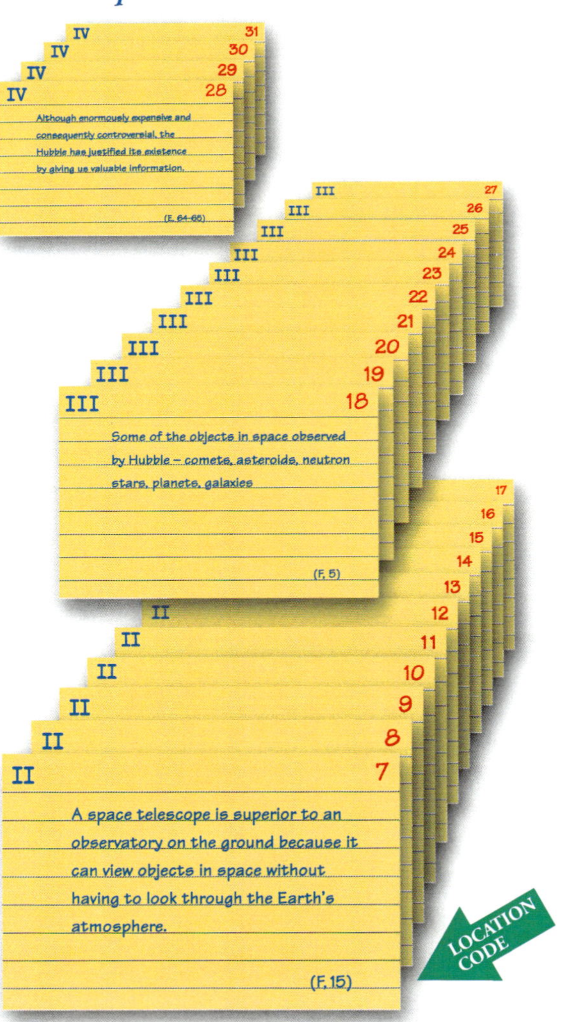

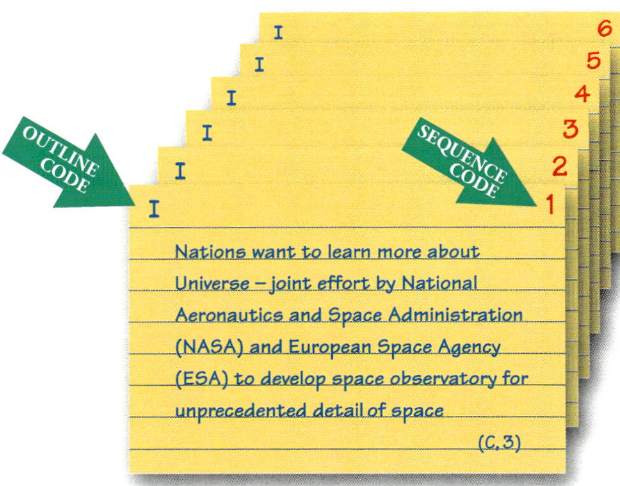

Research Papers

9. Write the first draft.

- Once the notecards are in sequence, begin writing the first draft.

- The paper begins with an <u>introductory paragraph</u> that presents the <u>topic</u>, provides some <u>background</u> information, and includes the <u>thesis statement</u> as the last sentence.

- A number of <u>body paragraphs</u> follow and make up the bulk of the paper. A body paragraph presents a <u>main idea</u>, which is supported by <u>details</u>. The main idea of a paragraph is written in the <u>topic sentence</u>.

- A <u>concluding paragraph</u> synthesizes the important main ideas in the paper. Written in a decisive and distinctive manner, it provides a <u>final perspective</u> on the thesis.

- Some students choose to develop their body paragraphs before writing the introduction. This strategy may help clarify their ideas and result in a stronger introduction.

- If the student is able to type easily, <u>input the text</u> into a word-processing program such as Microsoft Word or WordPerfect.

- Use the <u>notecards to create text</u> for the paper. The basic structure is already in place because the notecards were written while using the outline and thesis statement as guides.

- Add <u>transitional text</u> around the notes for flow and cohesion.

- <u>Cite sources</u> while writing, which is easy to do because the notecards have been coded.

- For specifics on formatting research papers and citing sources, use the teacher's recommendations, or refer to <u>formal guidelines</u> (MLA, APA, Chicago).

- Use the <u>automatic footnote</u> or <u>endnote</u> features provided in the computer software.

- Some students concentrate on <u>writing techniques</u> (vocabulary, transition, mechanics) in developing their first draft. Others prefer to get their ideas down and make improvements and corrections when revising and editing.

See Sample J.

J: Written Drafts – Paragraph Formats

INTRODUCTORY PARAGRAPH

OPENING SENTENCE – ideally, an attention-grabber that is a fact, quotation, or declaration about the topic

FOLLOWING SENTENCES
- include facts about the topic
- supply background information
- lead up to the thesis statement

THESIS STATEMENT – a sentence that identifies the purpose and point of view of the paper

BODY PARAGRAPHS

TOPIC SENTENCE* – presents a main idea

FOLLOWING SENTENCES – details that support the main idea in a topic sentence (description, explanation, and/or discussion)

ENDING SENTENCE – depends upon the way a paragraph is structured and the way the information unfolds

CONCLUDING PARAGRAPH

OPENING SENTENCE – makes a bold statement about the topic that brings the reader back to the focus of the paper

FOLLOWING SENTENCES
- describe where the paper has led the reader by synthesizing the important main ideas
- express a realization about the thesis
- suggest broader implications

ENDING SENTENCE
- concludes the paper in a decisive and interesting manner
- may parallel the opening sentence of an introduction – with a provocative quotation, for example
- may propose a course of action, a solution to a problem, or a question for further study

** A <u>topic sentence</u> may appear in the beginning, middle, or end of a paragraph.*

10. <u>Revise and edit</u> for the final draft.

- It is essential to revise, edit, and proofread. After making the effort to outline, research, take notes, and draft text, abandoning ship at this critical stage would be unfortunate.

- Before making corrections, <u>save</u> the first draft: Hubble_DRAFT. Then <u>rename</u> the document: Hubble_FINAL, and begin the revision process.

- Read the paper silently and <u>out loud</u>.

- <u>Scrutinize</u> the research paper for content, organization, language usage, mechanics.

- First, read for <u>content</u> – the quality, breadth, and depth of information. Even at this stage, sentences can be added to round out the paper.

- Then, check for <u>organization</u>. Read the topic sentences consecutively to determine whether the paragraphs are sequenced in an effective manner.

- Look at <u>language usage</u> and <u>mechanics</u>: transitional words and phrases; descriptive vocabulary; correct grammar, spelling, punctuation, capitalization.

- Use <u>computer tools</u> provided by word-processing programs – <u>grammar and spelling checkers</u>, for example – but do so carefully as some corrections may not be applicable. Also, take advantage of the <u>dictionary</u>, <u>thesaurus</u>, <u>word-count</u>, and <u>footnote</u> features.

- Memorize and use computer <u>keystrokes</u> to cut, copy, paste, and undo. This saves time when editing a paper.

- Follow the <u>documentation</u> rules that the teacher provides. If none are provided, use formal guidelines (MLA, APA, Chicago).

- The student must always be aware of the <u>teacher's expectations</u>. Is a <u>checklist</u> provided for self-evaluation? If not, use the sample shown here.

See Samples K, L, & M.

K: Checklist for Revising and Editing

THESIS

- Do I have a clear, well-written thesis statement with a specific point of view?
- Did I support the thesis statement throughout my paper?

CONTENT

- Do I have sufficient information?
- Do enough details support each of my main ideas?

ORGANIZATION

- Do I have an introduction and conclusion?
- Do my body paragraphs progress in a logical sequence?

LANGUAGE

- Have I used transitional words and phrases, descriptive vocabulary, and a variety of sentence types?
- Have I avoided repetitive words and phrases (unless used intentionally)?

MECHANICS

- Have I used correct grammar, spelling, punctuation, and capitalization?

DOCUMENTATION

- Are my sources documented correctly?

PRESENTATION

- Is the format of my paper correct?
- Have I put a heading on my paper?
- Have I made a cover and/or title page?

L: Keystrokes for Easy Editing

WINDOWS	KEYSTROKES	MAC	KEYSTROKES
CUT	CONTROL – X	CUT	COMMAND – X
COPY	CONTROL – C	COPY	COMMAND – C
PASTE	CONTROL – V	PASTE	COMMAND – V
UNDO	CONTROL – Z	UNDO	COMMAND – Z

M: Final Draft (Introduction)

OPENING SENTENCE

Many nations share the desire to learn more about the Universe. The joint effort made by the National Aeronautics and Space Administration (NASA) and the European Space Agency (ESA) to explore space in unprecedented detail was made possible through the development of a powerful space observatory. Named after Edwin P. Hubble, a famous American astronomer (Chaisson 3), ✱ the Hubble Space Telescope became "our new window on the universe" (qtd. in Fischer 25). While orbiting the Earth, this reflector telescope uses mirrors to observe light from the great "celestial dome" (Docherty 50; Chaisson 3). In spite of "a flaw in its main mirror," the Hubble has succeeded in making remarkable discoveries before and especially after its repair ("April"). **The Hubble Space Telescope is a prime example of technological progress in our space program, which has led to new advances in science.**

THESIS STATEMENT

✱*Parenthetical citations refer to the list of works cited at the end of a paper.*

(M: Notecards for Introduction)

I   1

Nations want to learn more about Universe – joint effort by National Aeronautics and Space Administration (NASA) and European Space Agency (ESA) to develop space observatory for unprecedented detail of space

(C, 3)

I   2

Hubble is named after Edwin P. Hubble, once an influential American astronomer.

(C, 3)

I   3

Hubble – "our new window on the universe" said by NASA launch commentator [indirect source]

(F, 25)

I   4

Hubble – reflector telescope that collects visible light with mirrors and produces images while in orbit

(D, 50)

I   6

Although "a flaw in its main mirror" was found, great discoveries were made before and especially after the repair.

(A)

I   5

"Overhead, the celestial dome pulsed eerily with scores of bright sources [. . .]," just waiting to be viewed by Hubble.

(C, 3)

11. Write a title.

- Write a concise title that suggests the <u>focus</u> of the research paper.

- At the same time, try to reflect the <u>scope</u> of the paper without repeating the thesis.

- For example, "The Hubble Space Telescope" does not narrow down the topic. Perhaps, "A Look at Our Universe through the Hubble Space Telescope" works better. Notice that the word "look" has a double meaning.

- Some students may wish to create a suitable <u>cover</u>. *See Sample N.*

N: Title and Cover

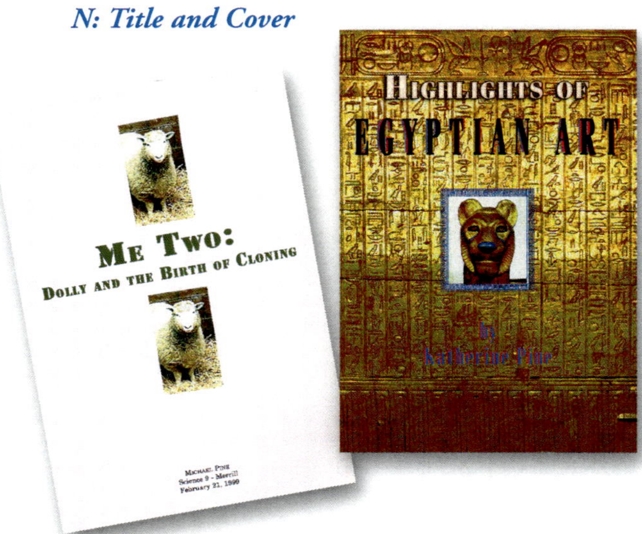

12. Prepare a final bibliography.

- Look through the <u>source cards</u>, and eliminate the ones not used in the research paper. <u>Alphabetize</u> the remaining cards according to the first letter of each entry. (The source cards were already written in the correct format for a bibliography.)

- <u>Entitle</u> a new page "Bibliography," "Works Cited," or" References," depending on the guidelines for documentation.

- <u>Transfer</u> the identifying information from the source cards.

- Pay attention to <u>formatting</u> (double-spacing, indenting, underlining). *See Sample O.*

O: Works Cited – MLA Style

Works Cited

"April 24 Marks a Triumphant Ten Years in Space for Hubble Space Telescope." 11 Apr. 2000. 14 Jan. 2001<http://oposite.stsci.edu/pubinfo/PR/2000/16/index.html>.

"Black Holes Shed Light on Galaxy Formation." 5 June 2000. 15 Jan. 2001<http://oposite.stsci.edu/pubinfo/PR/2000/22/index.html>.

Chaisson, Eric J. <u>The Hubble Wars: Astrophysics Meets Astropolitics in the Two-Billion-Dollar Struggle over the Hubble Space Telescope</u>. Cambridge: Harvard UP, 1998.

Docherty, Paul, ed. <u>The Visual Dictionary of the Universe</u>. London: DK, 1993.

Field, George B., and Donald Goldsmith. <u>The Space Telescope: Eyes Above the Atmosphere</u>. Chicago: Contemporary, 1989.

Fischer, Daniel, and Hilmar Duerbeck. <u>Hubble Revisited: New Images from the Discovery Machine</u>. Trans. Helmut Jenkner. New York: Copernicus, 1998.

Peterson, Carolyn Collins, and John C. Brandt. <u>Hubble Vision: Further Adventures with the Hubble Space Telescope</u>. 2nd ed. Cambridge: Cambridge UP, 1998.

Scott, Elaine. <u>Adventure in Space: The Flight to Fix the Hubble</u>. New York: Hyperion, 1995.

13. Look at another <u>introduction</u>.

- This introductory paragraph is from a <u>history paper</u> entitled, "The Impact of World War II on the Development of Fashion."

- The introduction opens with an engaging quotation that introduces the subject and continues with information that narrows down the topic and leads to a well-developed <u>thesis statement</u>. *See Sample P.*

14. Look at another <u>body paragraph</u>.

- This body paragraph is from a <u>biology paper</u> entitled, "Me Two: Dolly and the Birth of Cloning." The title is both informative and clever.

- The <u>detailed information</u> is described in a way that sustains the reader's interest. *See Sample Q.*

15. Look at another <u>conclusion</u>.

- This concluding paragraph is from a <u>science paper</u> entitled, "Environment Matters in Madagascar." The title cleverly employs a double meaning for the word "Matters."

- The conclusion <u>reviews</u> where the paper has led the reader and <u>validates</u> the thesis. *See Sample R.*

Sample: 9th-Grade Biology Paper

Q: Body Paragraph

TOPIC SENTENCE

Dolly was born on July 6, 1996, at 5:00 p.m., the most famous sheep to enter this world. She was 14.5 pounds, covered in grayish-white wool, and had a very white face. She looked like most other lambs in Scotland, but her birth marked a milestone in scientific history.[12] * Dolly was the identical twin of her own mother, the sheep whose udder cell was used as the transplant. **Ian Wilmut named**

ENDING SENTENCE

the lamb Dolly after the famous singer Dolly Parton, also well-known for her "mammary glands."[13]

Sample: 12th-Grade History Paper

P: Introduction

OPENING SENTENCE

Louis XIV was quoted as saying, "Fashion is the mirror of history." Throughout the civilized world, major events have affected and molded fashion of the day.[1] * This observation was particularly evident in the countries of France, England, and the United States during World War II.[2]

THESIS STATEMENT

In France, the war served to heighten the ingenuity of fashion designers while England's interest in fashion diminished, and America reacted by launching a new industry.

Sample: College-Level Science Paper

R: Conclusion

OPENING SENTENCE

Many nations, large and small, have begun to participate in the management of their natural resources. Due to an increase in awareness and education, the routine destruction of natural habitats has lessened. Although this progress is encouraging, care must be taken to ensure that employment opportunities remain available in local communities. The country of Madagascar has been involved in numerous environmental programs that have helped evade the destruction of its ecosystems ("Madagascar's"). At the same time, according to Russell A. Mittermeier, president of Conservation International, "President Ratsiraka understands that the intact biodiversity of his nation represents a strong competitive advantage in economic terms [. . .]" (qtd. in "Madagascar's").

ENDING SENTENCE

Exemplifying the balance between preservation and productivity, this small country has acted on the need to protect its biological wealth while also improving human conditions.

* *This <u>note number</u> refers to an endnote or a footnote. When inputting text on the computer, the student can use the superscript type style to make a small, raised number or learn to use the automatic footnote or endnote features.*

> **"It annoys me when I get good grades on content but lose credit on writing."**

Most subjects require written work. From book reports to lab reports, attending to written expression along with content is necessary. The way a writer expresses ideas can make a significant difference to the reader. Use this section to help improve writing skills.

1. Use an appropriate <u>writing style</u>.

- Write in <u>standard English</u> for <u>formal academic</u> writing assignments (reports, essays, research papers).

- Students today are accustomed to the personal, casual, shorthand language of blogging, emailing, instant messaging, texting, and tweeting. They must make a <u>concerted effort to shift</u> from that informal style to formal, academic writing – with correct <u>grammar</u>, <u>sentence structure</u>, <u>punctuation</u>, <u>capitalization</u>.

- Be aware of the inclination to lapse into an informal style.

  <u>Refrain from using slang</u> and conversational language – "okay," "pretty sure," "the thing is."

  <u>Do not use contractions or abbreviate words</u> – "don't," "2nd" "it's."

  <u>Avoid first-person commentary</u> and announcing the topic of a paper –"I am going to write about," "This essay will concentrate on," "The goal of this report is."

- <u>Creative writing</u> can incorporate an <u>informal style</u>. Conversational language is often necessary to develop convincing stories, journal entries, plays. *See Samples A & B.*

B: Creative Writing
Middle School: English – Play

Seth: Yeah, they beat us 68-65. It was close 'til the last minute.

Jeff: Sorry I couldn't make it.

Malik: That's OK (motioning to the basket). Hey, ya got time to shoot a few?

A: Formal Academic Writing
Middle School: Social Studies – Report

There was no tradition of landscape painting in America before the 1800s. The first artist to paint the beauty of the American landscape was Thomas Cole, an Englishman. He was the leader of what became the Hudson River School of Art, which flourished between 1825 and the late 1800s. Included in this group were painters who lived in the northeastern part of the United States, along the Hudson River. Frederic Church, a student of Thomas Cole, was the most famous Hudson River painter.

High School: History – Research Paper

Unions are organizations that have been developed to protect the rights of workers; however, it remains unclear to what extent they have actually produced results. Tactics such as debating with the use of an impartial party or meeting to air grievances are employed to solve differences between unions and businesses (Nyland 1).

College: Education – Research Paper

The first video game was introduced in the early 1970s. Since then, electronic gaming has burgeoned into the "medium of choice" for current generations. For decades, psychologists, researchers, and educators have engaged in feverish debates over the impact of video games and other virtual media on adolescents. It is widely agreed that video game play affects many aspects of adolescent development, including identity formation, visual and spatial skills, attention, violence desensitization, gender, and most of all, learning and education. The extent of this influence on adolescent development coupled with its predominance make video gaming an important topic in the field of education: How do video games impact adolescent learning? Could video games be adopted in the classroom to improve schooling?

Writing Techniques

2. Expand vocabulary.

- Use specific and descriptive vocabulary.

- Choose vocabulary that corresponds to the subject.

- Use words that capture the intended meaning and fit the context of the writing.

- Avoid showy words if simpler, more direct words will work as well.

- Use a thesaurus and dictionary to find just the right word. On the computer, learn the keystrokes that access these word-finders.

- Vary vocabulary. Avoid repeating words at close intervals unless repetition is needed for clarity or emphasis.
  See Samples C, D, & E.

3. Check the use of nouns and pronouns.

- A reader may become confused if a pronoun can refer to more than one noun.

- Make sure a pronoun clearly refers to the noun it replaces.

- In the following example, to whom the pronoun *he* refers is unclear:

  "Babe Ruth is sometimes compared to Ted Williams, but he never accomplished a .400 annual batting average."

- The sentence is clearer when written as follows:

  "Babe Ruth is sometimes compared to Ted Williams, but Ruth never accomplished a .400 annual batting average."

4. Be concise.

- While expanding vocabulary is important, wordiness must be controlled.

- Write text that is essential for the purpose of an assignment.

- Try to use the fewest words possible to express an idea completely.

- Avoid talking around a subject. Try to find specific, descriptive words that enhance meaning. For example, "eating foods regularly that are good for the body" is acceptable, but "healthy eating habits" is more concise.

- Repeat text only to emphasize or summarize.

C: Direct Words/Terms Specific to Subject
College: Physiology – Research Paper

Sensory receptors detect physical changes that cause electrical discharges. The nerve impulses are then sent to the brain via the spinal cord. Neurotransmitters cross synapses to allow communication between nerves (Fox, 1999, p.262).

High School: English – Mock Debate

Danius Delphinus was the first witness called for the prosecution. His testimony laid the groundwork for the case. Danius alleged to have heard Socrates urging two of his students to rebel against the government with the use of force. Once this information came to the floor, the entire case seemed to revolve around it.

D: Descriptive Writing
High School: English – Journal Entry

I wandered down the stairs to see if my snake, Old King Cole, was making progress with his meal. I brought my cat along for company. The cat and I stared with morbid fascination as Cole swallowed the tail of the dead mouse, like a child slurps a strand of spaghetti.

High School: English – Memoir

With anticipation, the second grade gathered around the stage of the chapel at St. Peter's School. I grabbed Alisha's hand, and she squeezed mine reassuringly. Loud groans filled the room as the smaller parts were assigned such as the mice, the pumpkins, and the dirty laundry. Prince Charming lifted his eyebrows in approval as his part was cast, and Marilyn chuckled about the role of Stepmother. When Alisha's part was announced, "Old Queen Ella, the Aged Cinderella," she mustered up a brave, half smile. I was still reeling from her disappointment when I heard my name called. I was Cinderella!

E: Repetition for Emphasis
High School: History – Research Paper

As the English economy gradually declined, unemployment and poverty gradually rose.

Writing Techniques

- Choosing the right or <u>best word</u> may take time, but the result is a concise, well-written paper.

- When a certain number of words or pages are required, continue to include <u>relevant</u> information. Do not pad the paper with nonessential text.

- To keep track of the paper's length, use the <u>word-count features</u> provided in word-processing tools.
  See Sample F.

5. Choose correct <u>verb tenses</u>.

- Use the verb tense that corresponds to the <u>time of action</u> (past, present, or future).

- <u>Shift tenses</u> when changes in time occur within the text.

- Otherwise, <u>be consistent</u>. Incorrect shifts in tense interfere with the reader's understanding.
  See Samples G & H.

6. Incorporate <u>quotations</u> effectively.

- Use quotations when an author's <u>exact words</u> capture the <u>essence</u> of important facts and ideas.

- <u>Weave</u> quotations into the text, so the flow of language is not interrupted.

- Set up quoted material with a <u>variety of verbs</u>.
  See Sample I.

7. Vary <u>verbs that signal quotations</u>.

- The verb <u>to say</u> (says, said, saying) can be used to set up quotations when an author or speaker is quoted in text or when writing dialogue.

  The use of the word say is sometimes necessary so as not to bias the reader – reporting for a newspaper, for example.

  However, when appropriate, choose a verb that is more indicative of the author's or speaker's <u>point of view</u>:

  Chaisson <u>acknowledged</u> that it "was one of the most exciting and turbulent times in the history of astronomy."

  "There is no silver bullet or easy remedy for this situation," <u>admitted</u> Thomas Kelly, a representative of the M.T.A.

F: Essential Information
College: Biology – Lab Report

The Green Fluorescent Protein (GFP) is a fundamental tool for following gene expression. Initially, two bacterial cultures were used: one for the isolation of GFP and the other for establishing a growth curve of E. coli.

G: Consistency of Verb Tense
Middle School: English – Essay

On one occasion, he <u>entered</u> an elevator and <u>became irritated</u> because a woman <u>looked</u> at his feet.

H: Shifts in Verb Tense
Middle School: Language Arts – Monologue

I <u>am</u> Bard, slayer of the evil dragon Smaug. I <u>am</u> a hero and <u>have become</u> King of the Lakemen. When I <u>slayed</u> the dragon, a new light <u>was shed</u> over our town – a light of freedom from fear. Now, the treasure <u>waits</u> unguarded for us <u>to claim</u> as our own.

I: Integration of Quotations
College: Psychology – Research Paper

Rauscher, Shaw, and Ky (1993) reported findings on the "Mozart Effect" (p. 611). Their experiment provides a possible answer to the question, "Does listening to classical music increase intelligence?" In an effort to explain their findings, Rauscher and Shaw (1998) proposed that enhancement occurs because of the brain activity represented by the "'trion' model of the cortex" (p. 835).

Writing Techniques

■ Set up <u>dialogue</u> with words that reflect feelings:

Sarah proudly displayed the purple, sequined dress. "Isn't it beautiful?" she <u>sighed</u>.

———

"How much do I owe you, Matt?" <u>asked</u> Mrs. Green. Standing tall in front of her diminutive figure, Matthew <u>answered</u>, "Nothing at all Mrs. Green. I'm glad to help."

———

He paused, gauged the height of the obstacle and prepared for the leap of a lifetime. Three, two, one … Henry hurtled down the homemade runway, his skates scraping across the pavement. Quickening his pace, he zeroed in on his target, took off – up, up and over – and landed right smack on his backside. "I did it. I did it!" Henry <u>shouted</u>, waving triumphantly to his friends on the sidelines. Picking himself up, he <u>muttered</u>, "Now, all I have to do is land on my feet."

See Samples J & K.

J: Verbs Instead of "Say"

High School: English – Essay

As the play progresses, Mr. Hale concludes that John is a decent man and should not be sentenced to death. While speaking with Elizabeth, he <u>argues</u>, "It is mistaken law that leads you to sacrifice" (132; act 4).

College: Russian Literature – Research Paper

Despite Busygin's exposure as an imposter at the end of the play, Serafanov still accepts him as a son, <u>exclaiming</u>, "You're a true Sarafanov! You're my son! And my favorite son, what's more!" (132).

K: List of <u>Verbs Instead of "Say"</u>

acknowledge	contend	imply	respond
add	continue	insist	state
admit	convey	maintain	suggest
affirm	declare	note	think
agree	deny	observe	write
argue	disagree	predict	———————
assert	dispute	profess	———————
believe	emphasize	propose	———————
claim	endorse	question	———————
comment	establish	reason	———————
conclude	explain	refute	———————
confess	illustrate	repeat	———————
confirm	imagine	report	———————

8. Use <u>transitional words and phrases</u>.

- Effective use of transition helps to produce <u>cohesive writing</u>.

- Transitional words and phrases can create a <u>flow</u> of thought between sentences and paragraphs, but do not overuse them.

- Introductory phrases usually require a comma, but a single word or very short phrase does not (unless it is confusing without it).

- Look at these two examples of transitional phrases that are <u>integrated into text</u>:

  <u>In spite of</u> setbacks, the workers encouraged the union to strike.

  Jenny turned in an extra-credit poster to bring up her grade, <u>and</u> she studied harder for the next test.

  See Samples L, M, N, & O.

Samples: Transitional Words and Phrases

L: Contrasting/Adding/Setting up Examples
Middle School: Science – Memoir

<u>Although</u> my Attention Deficit Disorder (ADD) is a significant problem, it <u>also</u> has benefits. <u>For instance</u>, in basketball, I notice everything that is going on.

M: Highlighting
College: Cognitive Development – Case Study

This thought process is an example of Piaget's concrete operational stage of thinking. <u>Interestingly</u>, halfway through our telephone interview, Eric interjected...

N: Setting up Examples/Showing Sequence
Middle School: Social Studies – Report

The Egyptians were skillful and diligent workers who used their brains as well as brawn to build the pyramids. <u>For example</u>, they discovered a way of using bricks to move the heavy stones needed for construction. <u>First</u>, they stirred a mixture of mud, barley, and water until it became a thick paste. <u>Then</u>, they placed the mixture into molds and let it dry in the sun. From these bricks, the Egyptians built ramps that helped them carry the huge stones up the pyramids.

*O: List of <u>Transitional Words and Phrases</u>**

<u>Setting Up Examples</u>	<u>Highlighting</u>	<u>Comparing</u>		
for example	above all	also	on the other hand	later
for instance	especially relevant	at the same time	whereas	presently
in fact	important to note	equally	yet	soon
specifically	interestingly	in the same way	**<u>Showing Sequence</u>**	subsequently
to illustrate	most of all	just as	finally	then
<u>Adding to Thoughts</u>	of major concern	just like	first	until
also	**<u>Drawing Conclusions</u>**	likewise	lastly	**<u>Showing Cause and Effect</u>**
and	accordingly	similarly	next	as a result
another	as a result	**<u>Contrasting</u>**	second	because
furthermore	consequently	although	subsequently	consequently
in addition	in conclusion	but	then	due to
moreover	therefore	despite	**<u>Indicating Time</u>**	in view of
	to summarize	however	afterward	otherwise
		in contrast	at last	since
		in spite of	before long	then
			in the past	therefore

**Some of these words and phrases overlap categories to express different concepts.*

9. Vary kinds of sentences.

- Be aware of <u>sentence structure</u> – simple, compound, complex, and compound-complex.

  A <u>simple sentence</u> has one independent clause:

  [1 INDEPENDENT CLAUSE] *"I have a dream."* – Martin Luther King

  [1 INDEPENDENT CLAUSE] *"Humans have a knack for choosing precisely the things that are worst for them."*
  – from The Sorcerer's Stone by J.K. Rowling

  A <u>compound sentence</u> has at least two independent clauses:

  [3 INDEPENDENT CLAUSES] *"Tell the truth, work hard, and* [Coordinating Conjunction] *come to dinner on time."* – Gerald R. Ford

  A <u>complex sentence</u> has one independent clause and at least one dependent clause:

  [1 INDEPENDENT CLAUSE / 1 DEPENDENT CLAUSE] *"I am always doing that which I cannot do, in order that I may learn how to do it."*
  – Pablo Picasso [Subordinating Conjunction]

  A <u>compound-complex sentence</u> has at least two independent clauses and at least one dependent clause: [Subordinating Conjunction]

  [1 INDEPENDENT CLAUSE / 1 DEPENDENT CLAUSE / 1 INDEPENDENT CLAUSE] *"I stopped believing in Santa Claus, when my mother took me to see him in a store, and he asked for my autograph."* – Shirley Temple [Coordinating Conjunction]

  (For more about conjunctions: Step 10)

- Use different <u>sentence lengths</u>.

  If sentences are all about the same length – short, long, or in-between – the main ideas and relationships between them may become unclear.

  Use a combination of sentence lengths to help make the content clear and interesting.

- Use different <u>sentence beginnings</u>.

  A common way to begin a sentence is with a <u>subject</u>:

  "A joke is a very serious thing." – Winston Churchill

  However, if all sentences in a paragraph begin with a subject, it seems monotonous.

  Consider beginning sentences with different parts of speech. For example, this sentence begins with a <u>prepositional phrase</u>:

  "For two days the earth drank the rain, until the earth was full." – John Steinbeck

  See Samples P, Q, & R.

P: Varied Sentence Structure
High School: English – Research Paper

Cultural messages on the rewards of being skinny and the penalties of obesity are everywhere. Even as this standard chips away at self-image and self-esteem, most women accept it as "the way things are." Weight concerns are so common among girls that they escape notice. Dieting is not considered abnormal behavior, even among women who are not overweight, but there is only a thin line that separates normal dieting from an eating disorder.

Q: Varied Sentence Length
High School: History – Research Paper

The Vietnam War was unpopular in the United States. It was the first televised war, and its visibility provoked many Americans to form strong opinions. Many concluded that it caused an unnecessary loss of lives. Moreover, with little connection to the Asian country halfway around the world, Americans believed that the U.S. should not have been involved in its affairs.[18]

R: Varied Sentence Beginnings
Middle School: Science – Report

<u>Commuters</u> who use the Tappan Zee Bridge between Rockland and Westchester Counties have been fed up with the delays, accidents, and unpleasant driving conditions caused by tremendous congestion. <u>As conditions worsened,</u> politicians proposed building a new bridge with more lanes for traffic.

10. Use <u>conjunctions</u> to make compound and complex sentences.

- A <u>compound sentence</u> is made up of <u>at least two independent clauses</u>.

  An <u>independent clause</u> can stand alone as a sentence.

  Independent clauses are connected by <u>coordinating conjunctions</u>.

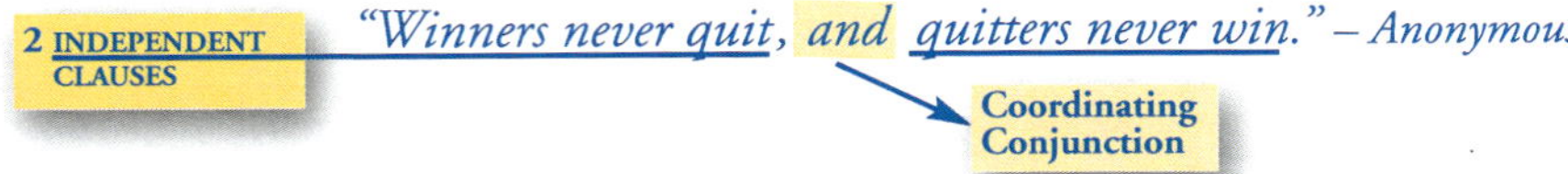

Refer to this <u>list of coordinating conjunctions</u>:

and	but	for	nor	or	so	yet

- A <u>complex sentence</u> is made up of <u>one independent clause and at least one dependent clause</u>.

  A <u>dependent clause</u> cannot stand alone as a sentence because it includes a <u>subordinating conjunction</u>.

Refer to this <u>list of common subordinating conjunctions</u>:

after	because	in order that	so that	until	whether
although	before	now that	than	when	while
as	even if	once	that	whenever	
as if	even though	provided	though	where	
as long as	if	rather than	till	whereas	
as though	if only	since	unless	wherever	

11. Avoid common mistakes in word usage.

- Students today rely on word-processing utilities, such as spelling and grammar checkers, that may fall short.

- Some words sound the same, have different meanings, and are spelled differently – **to and too:**

  "It is never too late to give up our prejudices." – Henry David Thoreau

- Some words sound similar but have different meanings. Often, they are mistakenly interchanged – **precede and proceed:**

  "Big thinking precedes great achievement." – Wilfred A. Peterson
  "Nature does not proceed by leaps and bounds." – Carl Linnaeus

- Words may have related meanings but distinct usage – **I and me:**

  "Somebody's boring me. I think it's me." – Dylan Thomas

- Students will undoubtedly hear and see these errors (and many more) committed routinely by people around them and in the broadcast and social media.

  Blogging, emailing, instant messaging, texting, and tweeting, have spawned shorthand styles that perpetuate the use of improper English.

  Students must differentiate informal communications from the proper English required when writing school assignments.

- Refer to this list of common mistakes in word usage.
  See Samples S, T, & U.

---

to, too, two

To means going toward or is part of a verb infinitive.

"It's a Long Way to Tipperary" – Song

"I refuse to join any club that would have me as a member." – Groucho Marx

Too means also.

"Weeds are flowers too, once you get to know them." – A. A. Milne

Two is the number after one.

"One today is worth two tomorrows."
– Benjamin Franklin

Samples: Common Mistakes in Word Usage

S: Words that Sound the Same

---

it's, its

It's is the contraction of it is.

"It's a Small World." – Song

Its is the possessive form of it.

"The whole is more than the sum of its parts."
– Aristotle

---

there, their, they're

There is the opposite of here.

"From there to here, from here to there, funny things are everywhere!" – Dr. Suess

Their is the possessive form of they.

"Cowards die many times before their deaths; the valiant never taste of death but once." – William Shakespeare

They're is the contraction of they are.

"Things are only impossible until they're not."
– Line from "Star Trek: The Next Generation"

---

who's, whose

Who's is the contraction of who is.

"Guess Who's Coming to Dinner?" – Movie

Whose is the possessive form of who.

"Whose Line Is It Anyway?" – TV Show

Writing Techniques

lose, loose

<u>Lose</u> means <u>something is lost</u>.

"No matter how good you are, you're going to <u>lose</u> one-third of your games."
– Tommy Lasorda

<u>Loose</u> means <u>not firmly fixed in place</u>.

"The ideal attitude is to be physically <u>loose</u> and mentally tight." – Arthur Ashe

who, that

Use <u>who</u> when referring to a <u>person</u>.

"He <u>who</u> laughs last, laughs best."
– Italian Proverb

Use <u>that</u> when referring to an <u>object</u>.

"A bank is a place <u>that</u> will lend you money if you can prove that you don't need it."
– Bob Hope

affect, effect

<u>Affect</u> is a verb meaning <u>to influence</u>.

"A chicken's prayer doesn't <u>affect</u> a hawk."
– African Proverb

<u>Effect</u> is a noun meaning <u>a result</u>.

"Hate and force cannot be in just a part of the world without having an <u>effect</u> on the rest of it." – Eleanor Roosevelt

i.e., e.g.

<u>i.e.</u> is a Latin abbreviation meaning <u>that is</u>.

The hotel is closed during the slow season (<u>i.e.</u>, from November through February).

<u>e.g.</u> is a Latin abbreviation meaning <u>for example</u>.

Eat more foods that contain fiber (<u>e.g.</u>, vegetables, fruit, and whole grains).

Use a comma after both of these abbreviations.

less, fewer

<u>Less</u> is used for things that <u>cannot be counted</u>.
<u>Fewer</u> is used for things that <u>can be counted</u>.

"If we had <u>less</u> statesmanship we could get along with <u>fewer</u> battleships."
– Mark Twain

that, which

Use <u>that</u> to introduce a clause that is <u>essential</u> for the meaning of a sentence.

"People will buy anything <u>that</u> is one to a customer." – Sinclair Lewis

Use <u>which</u> to introduce a clause that is <u>not essential</u> for the meaning of a sentence.

"My heart, <u>which</u> is so full to overflowing, has often been solaced and refreshed by music when sick and weary."
– Martin Luther

Use commas to set off the nonessential clause.

lay, lie

<u>Lay</u> in the present tense means <u>to place</u>.
<u>Lie</u> in the present tense means <u>to recline</u>.

"When it comes to my own turn to <u>lay</u> my weapons down, I shall do so with thankfulness and fatigue, and whatever be my destiny afterward, I shall be glad to <u>lie</u> down with my fathers in honor."

– Robert Louis Stevenson

a, an

Use <u>a</u> before a word starting with a <u>consonant sound</u>.

"To Kill <u>a</u> Mockingbird" – Book

Use <u>an</u> before a word starting with a <u>vowel sound</u>.

"The value of <u>an</u> idea lies in the using of it."
– Thomas A. Edison

BIBLIOGRAPHY AND SUGGESTED REFERENCES

Aaron, Jane E. *The Little, Brown Compact Handbook.* 4th ed. New York: Addison-Wesley Longman, 2001.

Gibaldi, Joseph. *MLA Handbook for Writers of Research Papers.* 5th ed. New York: Modern Language Association of America, 2000.

Strunk, William, and E. B. White. *The Elements of Style.* 4th ed. New York: Longman, 2000.

University of Chicago Press. *The Chicago Manual of Style.* 16th ed. Chicago: University of Chicago Press, 2010.

REPRINTED OR PARAPHRASED EXCERPTS

Blase, K., R. Wagner, and H. B. Clark. *SODAS Framework Personnel Training Module.* Tampa, FL: Louis de la Parte Florida Mental Health Institute, University of South Florida, 2005.

BSCS. *Biological Science: An Ecological Approach.* 7th ed. Dubuque, IA: Kendall/Hunt, 1992.

Cole, Joanna. *Norma Jean, Jumping Bean.* New York: Random House, 1987.

Davidson, James West, and John E. Batchelor. *The American Nation.* Englewood Cliffs, NJ: Prentice Hall, 1991.

Douglass, Frederick "What the Black Man Wants" (speech). *The Life and Writings of Frederick Douglass.* vol. 4, edited by Philip S. Foner. New York: International Publishers, 1950.

Dubowski, Cathy East, and Mark Dubowski. *Cave Boy.* New York: Random House, 1988.

Garraty, John A. *The Story of America.* Austin: Holt, Rinehart and Winston, 1994.

Holtzclaw, Fred, Linda Cronin Jones, and Steve Miller. *Science Explorer: Environmental Science.* Needham, MA: Prentice Hall, 2000.

Kassirer, Norma. *Magic Elizabeth.* New York: Scholastic Book Services, 1966.

Milton, Joyce. *Dinosaur Days.* New York: Random House, 1985.

Morrison, Earl S., Alan Moore, Nan Armour, Allan Hammond, John Haysom, Elinor Nicoll, and Muriel Smyth. *Scienceplus: Technology and Society.* Austin: Holt, Rinehart and Winston, 1993.

Peck, M. Scott. *The Road Less Traveled: A New Psychology of Love, Traditional Values and Spiritual Growth.* New York: Simon and Schuster, 1978.

Shakespeare, William. *Romeo and Juliet.* Edited by Barbara A. Mowat and Paul Werstine. New York: Washington Square Press, 1992.

Thoreau, Henry D. *Walden.* Edited by Jeffrey S. Cramer. New Haven: Yale University Press, 2004.